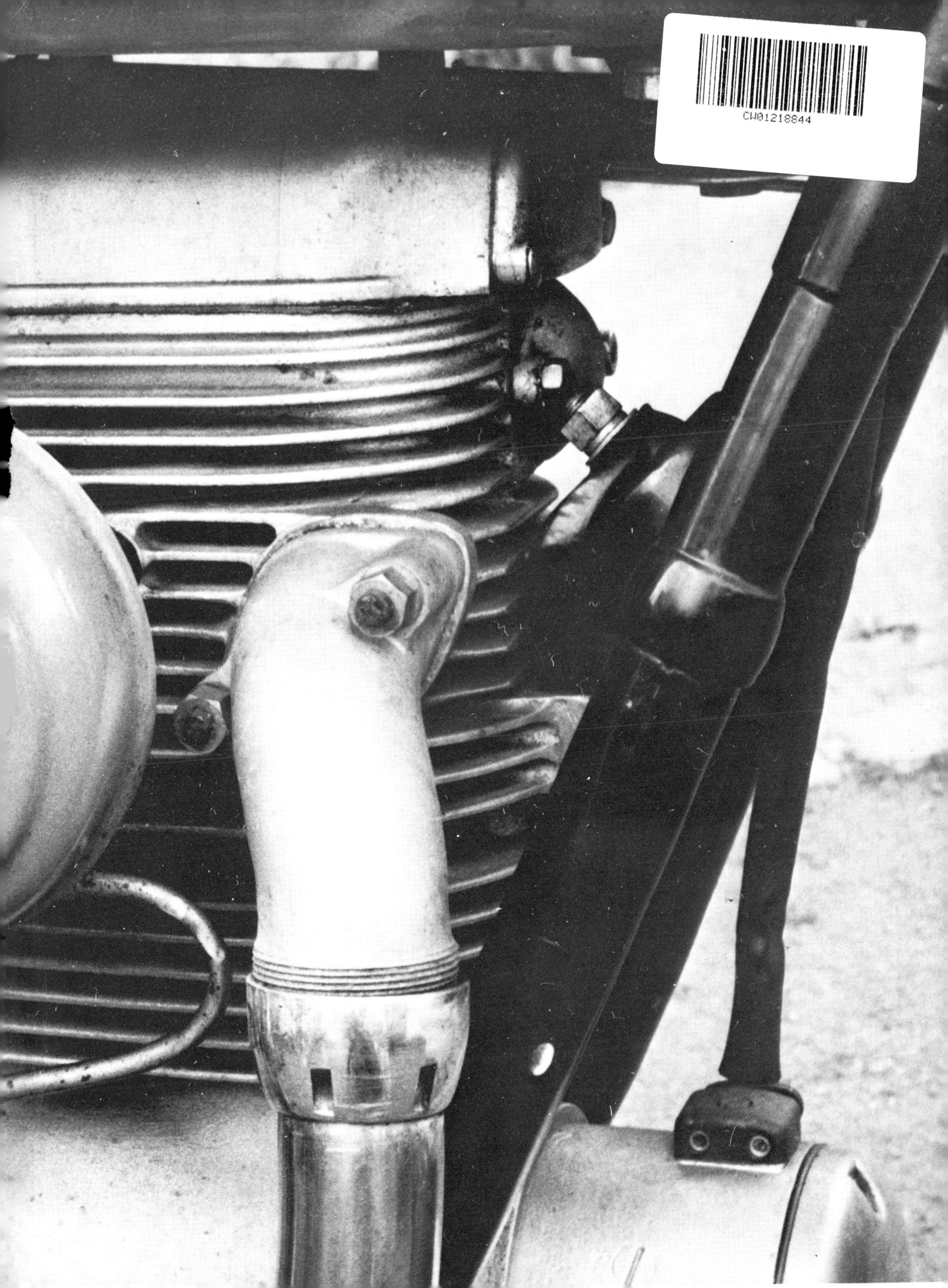

SUNBEAM S7 & S8

Robert Cordon Champ

CONTENTS

FOREWORD	4
HISTORY	5
EVOLUTION	9
ROAD TESTS	16
OWNER'S VIEW	23
BUYING	25
CLUBS SPECIALISTS & BOOKS	27
PHOTO GALLERY	29

Foulis

Haynes

Titles in the *Super Profile* series

BSA Bantam (F333)
MV Agusta America (F334)
Norton Commando (F335)
Honda CB750 sohc (F351)
Sunbeam S7 & S8 (F363)
BMW R69 & R69S (F387)

Austin-Healey 'Frogeye' Sprite (F343)
Ferrari 250GTO (F308)
Ford GT40 (F332)
Jaguar D-Type & XKSS (F371)
Jaguar Mk 2 Saloons (F307)
Lotus Elan (F330)
MGB (F305)
Morris Minor & 1000 (ohv) (F331)
Porsche 911 Carrera (F311)

B29 Superfortress (F339)
Boeing 707 (F356)
Harrier (F357)

Further titles in this series will be published at regular intervals. For information on new titles please contact your bookseller or write to the publisher.

ISBN 0 85429 363 9

A FOULIS Motorcycling Book

First published July 1983

© **Haynes Publishing Group**

All rights reserved. No part of this book may be reproduced or transmitted in any form or by any means, electronic or mechanical, including photocopying, recording or by any information storage or retrieval system, without written permission from the publisher.

Published by:
Haynes Publishing Group
Sparkford, Yeovil,
Somerset BA22 7JJ

Distributed in USA by:
Haynes Publications Inc.
861 Lawrence Drive, Newbury Park, California 91320, USA

Editor: Jeff Clew
Cover design: Rowland Smith
Page Layout: Gill Carroll
Colour photography: Andrew Morland
Road tests: Courtesy of *Motor Cycling* and *Motor Cycle* (IPC)
Printed in England by: J.H.Haynes & Co. Ltd

Super Profile

FOREWORD

In 1945 there came the first rumours of a radically different motorcycle from the great BSA company of Birmingham, England. In the immediate post-war period anything new was indeed exciting, so many motorcycle factories, including BSA, having merely recommenced production of their 1939 ranges which were snapped up by a bike-starved population. Indeed, it may be said that there were only three new motorcycles designed after the war, so complacent had the chiefs of the industry become. These three were the Ariel Leader, Sunbeam S7 and Velocette LE, and the first to appear was the distinctive Sunbeam. Although the basic concept of the S7 resulted from design work done in another country, the machine itself was immediately noticed by both the motorcycling and non-motorcycling public, and the resultant special status has survived, making the S7 and the later S8 prominent amongst the machines about which older people say 'I remember those ...'

In reality, any book about BSA's Sunbeam motorcycles is a book about three rather differing bikes. The original S7 of 1947 was put into production with several in-built disadvantages and suffered accordingly. The advent of the S7 de luxe in 1949 heralded a complete re-design of the original, and the later bikes were very different in both basic and detail design and construction. The third model of the Sunbeam trio, the S8, modified the original design yet again into something nearer to the ordinary motorcycle of the day.

In perhaps typical BSA fashion, the S7 de luxe and S8 were then allowed to soldier on, almost unchanged and undeveloped, until they were outclassed by newer designs from rival makers. The Sunbeam had always had an unfortunate reputation for unreliability, in my experience likely to be due to unsympathetic ownership and service, and this did not help sales in the nineteen fifties. There was, however, a solid and faithful band of enthusiasts for the shaft-drive twins and their tradition has continued.

In the late 'fifties and 'sixties the factory was able to provide spares and service but one firm which started in business at that time, Stewart Engineering, at first in Putney and now at Market Harborough, has become universally known for helping the Sunbeam enthusiasts. Their efforts have kept the bikes on the road, where they belong.

This Super Profile makes no attempt to be an encyclopaedia about these fine motorcycles but is a friendly and, I hope, unbiased look through the eyes of an enthusiast for Sunbeams of all types who believes that these bikes should not become 'investments' (whatever that means) but should be used.

I would like to thank the following for their help. Without the aid of a large number of people, the enthusiast could not complete a rebuild or belong to a club and the same applies to the motorcycle writer. In my case my thanks are due to the owners who made their machines available for photography and to those who were able to help me on minor points.

The author is also most indebted to *Motor Cycle Weekly* who generously made available their major road-tests of the Sunbeams from the pages of *Motor Cycle* and *Motor Cycling*.

When all the scribbling was finished, Joan Hawes made sense of the handwriting, as she has so often done, and Jeff Clew had the unenviable task of writing letters and directing the operation.

Lastly, Jacqueline my wife, with James and Gemma, who tolerated my cries of 'Shut up, I'm trying to write!' and the frequent and interminable calls and piles of correspondence from Sunbeam enthusiasts, the magnetos in the wardrobe and all the other disadvantages of belonging to the family of a motorcyclist.

Robert Cordon Champ

Super Profile

HISTORY

Family Tree

The trade mark of 'The Sunbeam' was originally that of a very high-grade bicycle made by John Marston Ltd. of Wolverhampton, in England's Black Country. John Marston was a craftsman and Master in the Victorian manner. He started as an apprentice to a Wolverhampton tinsmith and finally returned as Master to this business. Able to do any job in the factory to as high a standard as any of his workforce, Marston was a hard man to please, but characteristically, paid excellent wages for good work.

In the late eighteen-eighties, Marston turned his hobby to advantage by starting production of a cycle in his tinplate and japanning works. At once a success, 'The Sunbeam' then acquired the 'Little Oil-bath Chaincase' totally enclosing the chain and chainwheels in a weather and dust-proof oil-bath. The Sunbeam soon became regarded as the best-constructed cycle of all as, indeed, it still remains. Marston's insistence on the finest possible construction allied to the best possible specification meant that the 'Golden Sunbeam' remained in production until 1936, so perfect that no-one could think of any worth-while improvements. Many are still in use after over half a century.

In 1900, at the age of sixty-four, Marston became interested in powered transport and produced two prototype cars, duly founding the Sunbeam Motor Car Co. Ltd. in 1905. Although the motorcycle should have been the logical step from the cycle, Marston disliked the frantic antics inseparable from the primitive, clutchless single-speeders of the day, refusing to make a motorcycle at all unless it could be ridden in a gentlemanly fashion.

In 1912 the first motorcycle was made, at the cycle works. A $2\frac{3}{4}$ hp (350cc) side valve, it was billed as 'The Gentleman's Machine', as indeed it was. Most of them were finished in the famous Sunbeam 'black and gold', using real gold leaf for the lining.

The Wolverhampton factory went on producing beautifully made single cylinder motorcycles after John Marston's death in 1918, at the age of eighty two. Some twin-cylinder models were made for sidecar use, but the characteristic Sunbeam was the side valve and overhead valve single, usually light and fast. Sunbeams won the TT in 1920 and 1922 and many, many races all over the world. Their chief tester, the legendary George Dance, made sprinting an almost entirely Sunbeam province in the early twenties, and the reputation of the factory was high when it became part of the ICI combine in 1928.

Two more TT wins, in 1928 and 1929 with Charlie Dodson, were to be Sunbeam's racing swansong. As the hand of ICI and the depression both grew tighter, 'The Sunbeam' shrank into becoming just another motorcycle, albeit still a very well made and finished one.

In September 1937, the motorcycle production and trade mark were sold to the London-based Associated Motor Cycles who had already swallowed Sunbeam's Wolverhampton rivals, AJS, and were to takeover many others. AMC continued to assemble Sunbeams from Wolverhampton parts but in 1939 displayed a new range of sporting singles, still in the characteristic black and gold. Excellent machines, well-made and reliable, these were to be in production for one season only, cut off by other events in 1939. AMC had also produced the Sunbeam cycles at Plumstead, seeing the cycle trade mark as more important than that of the motorcycle, at least at first. The singles were listed for 1940, but the last Sunbeam actually made was a V-twin sidecar-wheel drive prototype for Army use. The arrival of the Jeep killed this.

In 1943 the thoughts of manufacturers began to turn towards the war's end and BSA decided to expand their cycle output to rival that of Raleigh. In pursuit of a trade mark, they approached AMC and a deal was struck whereby the cycle and motorcycle manufacturing rights went to Birmingham, although the Sunbeam singles never re-appeared. Sunbeam Cycles Ltd was incorporated on 25th November 1943.

As BSA thought about post-war work, the Sunbeam trade mark assumed more importance and it was decided to use it on a completely new twin-cylinder model which would carry on the traditions of the great John Marston and become 'The Gentleman's Machine'.

Concept

During the war it was standard practice for captured enemy vehicles to be evaluated by makers of similar bikes or cars, tanks or 'planes, in England. BSA had been given a stream of captured Zundapp, NSU, BMW and other German bikes and the decision was

5

Super Profile

made to examine two of them very carefully with a view to a post-war range. One was the DKW RT125 which, after the war, became the famous BSA 'Bantam', (copied in many other countries) and is the subject of another Super Profile. The other was the BMW R75 Army model of 1941.

The BMW was a flat-twin ohv heavyweight with an integral drive to a sidecar wheel. The complete outfits were used in all campaigns and still appear in films today. BSA were impressed with the comfort and handling of the model in both solo and sidecar forms and decided to copy it. Understandably, BSA felt that an ohv flat-twin would shout 'copy' from the rooftops to customers who would not be very pro-German in 1946 so a search was made for a suitable engine to fit the running gear.

For the re-design BSA secured the services of Erling Poppe. Poppe had been connected with the motor trade for many years, his family's firm of White and Poppe making the engines for the original 'Bullnose' Morris. Poppe had designed motorcycles in the twenties as a partner in Packman and Poppe of Coventry, who made conventional machines powered by proprietary engines. After the death of his partner, Erling Poppe had gone into the heavy vehicle field until called back to motorcycles by BSA.

Poppe looked long and hard at the BMW and decided that a complete re-design rather than a slavish copy was the answer. The engine he chose to develop was one that had been lying around the BSA experimental shop since 1932, known as the 'LAT' for 'Line-Ahead Twin'. This, too, served only as the starting point for Poppe's ideas.

By 1946 the new motorcycle was being tested, in prototype form, under the BSA staff. The work was not done in Birmingham but in BSA's other factory at Redditch in Worcestershire, and all the development and testing as well as the actual production was carried out there.

A number of design changes had taken place, the most obvious, besides the engine type, being the early replacement of the BMW hypoid rear-drive unit with a worm and wheel one. This was to suit available production facilities within the BSA group whose Daimler and Lanchester arm had used this type of rear-axle drive for years. The in-line twin engine was carried in a double cradle frame similar to that of the BMW, and like the BMW, the S7 had robust telescopic forks up front – an area in which the German industry led the British one – and a rigid rear end. The wheels and tyres were similarly constructed to those on the BMW and just as massive, being interchangeable and having Dunlop block-tread 4.75 x 16 inch ELP tyres. The brakes were of typically German type with the front operating mechanism enclosed in the brake plate casting and the handlebars were of the 'clean' type with the cables running through them from the 'inverted' levers, again just like those on the BMW. There was, at last, a proper built-in tax-disc holder and a ratchet-held combination prop and centre stand.

Initially, prototypes were constructed to various specifications, one of the first having a rigid rear-end with the frame looping round the rear-drive as on the BMW. The engine seems to have originally been intended for high performance, featuring a cross-flow cylinder-head with hemispherical combustion chambers and valves inclined at 45°. The engine was of the single overhead camshaft type with a tremendously strong and rigid bottom end, the crankcase being a one-piece alloy casting with iron cylinder liners and the dynamo driven straight off the front of the crankshaft.

The transmission avoided having a kick start at right-angles to the bike, common on in-line crankshaft bikes, and was well designed and robustly constructed.

The front tyre was soon changed for a 4.50-16 ribbed cover to remedy the uncertain steering. This robbed the Sunbeam of any hope of making use of the interchangeable wheels and the only explanation for the step of putting heavy covers on both wheels was that most R75 BMW's were so fitted – for sidecar use, not solo riding. Perhaps no-one at Redditch ever rode a BMW solo for very long.

The 'S7' – a designation whose derivation remains obscure unless it merely related to the fact that the seventh Sunbeam prototype was the one chosen for such productionising as BSA ever gave to anything – was an unsatisfactory motorcycle, even for a prototype. The engine was high-revving, the exceptionally short stroke and stiff crankshaft making this inevitable. It produced plenty of power, good for over 90 mph, but at the cost of excessive vibration, serious wear in the worm drive unit, and a seemingly serious 'torque reaction' if the prototype was opened up or shut down at any speed. The power delivery was 'peaky' and when the power came in, the bike twitched to the right sufficiently to make going up through the gears a hazardous affair. At least one rider was propelled inexorably off the road as he attempted to accelerate into a left-hand curve.

The vibration was remarkable. An often told tale is that of Charles Markham, *Motor Cycling's* well-liked journalist, going to Triumph's Meriden factory on a later, lower-powered S7 and lending the plot to Ernie Nott, the hard-riding TT man who was then a Triumph tester. Ernie set off, using the Sunbeam's revs to the full in finest Isle of Man style. After a while, when there was no sign of Ernie, faces began to fall, not least Charlie Markham's. At last, the Sunbeam re-appeared, at walking pace, with the engine hanging in the frame. The vibration had broken all the mounting bolts, and specials had to be made in the experimental shop at Triumph before Markham could take the bike back to Redditch. The worm rear drive lasted only a few miles under this treatment, being a transmission more suited to low power and low revolutions. After two or three hundred miles it began to knock, the oil resembling gold paint with the ground bronze particles released into it, which themselves prompted yet more wear.

At this point, the decision was made to revise the engine, rather than the rear drive. The deciding factor was the machine's handling, which was hardly that of a sports model. It was thought that the three major problems would disappear with less power available. The original engine also had a poorly-designed cylinder head, which allowed large quantities of oil to collect round the rockers, starving the remainder of the bearings and resulting in their spectacular failure.

The famous George Dance, of Sprint Sunbeam fame and the genius of competition development at the old Wolverhampton factory, was invited to test a number of prototypes. Written up in the motorcycling press and accompanied by photographs, the old racer's comments are said to have been most unfavourable. Since Dance had developed road motorcycles weighing under two hundred and fifty pounds which handled as though on rails, it is not surprising that 4.75-16 tyres under four hundredweight of metal failed to impress him.

The testers, too, found the prototypes odd and rather fragile, prone to breakdown, with any sort of puncture being rather dangerous. The front forks were revised after a couple of frightening breakages and the factory was in some trouble with its Sunbeam flagship.

A different cylinder head was designed to fit on to the original crankcase – the fit was then by no means exact and the cam chain ran rather close to the castings, the new pattern leaving rather untidy 'edges' between the two castings. The flat combustion chambers and in-line valves cut the power to 23.6 bhp (a factory figure) which helped the handling, reduced the rear-drive wear and emasculated the performance, leaving the S7 on the verge of being underpowered, which was to hinder it in the sales stakes.

The unit was also tilted downwards at the rear by 3° which did not help with the shaft-drive angles on the plunger-sprung prototypes. Iron 'elbows' linked engine to exhaust pipe, the exhaust pipe pattern remaining unchanged. In this form, the torque reaction had largely gone. Vibration was still a major problem but it was never seriously tackled at the prototype stage. BSA always had a strongly hierarchical management structure, intensified under Sir Bernard Docker and his publicity-conscious wife, whose gold-plated Daimlers were to become a feature of post-war motor shows. The road testers were pretty near the bottom of the heap and if their comments did not fit in with what management wanted to hear, they were ignored. In this form, the S7 was put into limited production and advertised, a batch being crated and sent to South Africa for police use during a Royal visit. It was only when they were returned as unridable that BSA's management conceded that the vibration might be a deterrent to sales. The engine mountings were changed from the normal motorcycle rigid mountings to flexible ones of rubber. This was achieved in a compromise fashion by making up a crudely welded steel mounting to isolate the gearbox from the frame and sandwiching between the two a rubber disc bonded to a steel mounting. At the front another rubber block was added to the mounting at the front of the block casting, and this further 'sandwich' fitted between the engine and a modified frame down-tube lug.

In order to limit sideways movement, the front through-bolt mounting was used to carry small rubber 'snubbers' fitting into the crankcase, with adjustable flat head bolts filling in the corresponding frame lugs. In order to preserve some frame rigidity, a crossbar was also held between the two side cradles of the frame at this point. The exhaust pipe moved with the engine and the now familiar length of flexible tubing was introduced, forward of the silencer.

It had been a long time since the first hints of the new machine had been put out, in June 1945, by the BSA publicity machine. Customer interest had been fired by articles in the two weekly magazines and by a form of 'customer research' dedicated to drumming up a market, but the long delay had cooled expectations.

On 7th March 1946 *Motor Cycling* were able to describe the S7 in rigid-engine form, referring to the forthcoming 'sports model' which was already, in reality, a dead letter. The report, by Graham Walker, commented on 'the performance which is deceptive because of its very smoothness', an example of the manufacturer-vetted journalistic optimism which was to enable British manufacturers to foist second-rate products on to so many ill-informed customers before the Japanese came.

It was not until October 1947 that a proper *Motor Cycle* road test of a revised, rubber-mounted Sunbeam could be found. The tester praises the unique features of the Sunbeam but is plainly uneasy about the handling. In March 1948, Charles Markham tested a production bike for *Motor Cycling* He praised the positive aspects of the bike like its integral controls and ratchet main/prop stand operated by foot pedal but was unhappy about the handling and the lack of oil pressure as soon as the sump level dropped – but generally gave a good report.

Super Profile

Production got under way and the S7 started to sell. At Redditch, Erling Poppe had been given fifteen minutes in which to clear out his desk and leave the organisation — going on to motorcycle design work for the ill-fated Douglas company — and a re-design of his S7 was contemplated.

At the 1948 Motor Cycle Show at Earls Court, the Sunbeam was featured prominently on an elaborate stand. One of the large, black bikes was presented to 'Monty' — Field Marshal The Viscount Montgomery of Alamein — one of the country's heroes in World War Two and a man to whom publicity came easily. What 'Monty' was supposed to do with the bike was a mystery since he was no motorcyclist, but James Leek, BSA's Managing Director, certainly got his money's worth of Sunbeam publicity. In fact the crush to see 'Monty's' Sunbeam was so great that the centrepiece of the firm's stand collapsed, fortunately without dropping an S7 on anyone.

The unfortunate Sunbeam was taken away to the Field Marshal's home where it joined various staff cars, his campaign caravan and other relics. Never ridden, it was acquired by a Motor Museum in Jersey after Montgomery's death.

Despite these efforts, the S7 was never a great success.

Super Profile

EVOLUTION

Sales reactions had shown that many prospective customers for a 'gentleman's machine' were turned away by the massive, weighty appearance of the S7 and so a lighter sports version was conjured up. The opportunity was taken to fit the new S8 more closely into BSA's other bike production by utilising standard parts from the 'A' twin and 'B' singles ranges and the S7 was likewise re-designed, losing the unique front and rear suspension, the ratchet stand, integral controls and under-engine mounting cradle. The engine and gearbox castings were revised to take built-in mounting lugs and also gained a reasonable oil capacity.

In 1949 the two new models burst upon an indifferent world. The initial production batch of less than 2,500 S7s laid down in 1946 had been sold, or scrapped at BSA, and the new bikes stood ready to redeem the poor reputation of 'The Sunbeam'. This had stemmed mainly from dealers whose mechanics had been unused to ohc-engined bikes which needed careful setting up, but there had been many genuine cases of engine damage on the old S7 due to lack of oil and the poor fit of the force-fit cylinder liners — this latter bother cured by the S7 de luxe and S8 being given dowelled, push-in liners.

The S7 was now called the S7 de luxe. At first glance the most noticeable change was the colour. Instead of Sunbeam's traditional black finish, the S7 was a sort of pea-green, labelled by BSA as Mist Green. Just why this awful shade was chosen is not clear but it did nothing for the look of the bike. Strangely, the S8 retained black as a finish, though it was never again available on the S7 much to its disadvantage for, as any schoolboy knows, objects look larger when painted in light colours. The S7 did not need to look any larger, and this deliberate break with the early S7 misfired badly with the buying public. BSA never changed the colour, which has led to speculation that only one batch of S7 mudguards were made.

The beautiful handlebars had also gone. Though the inverted levers were awkward and expensive to make, they do fit a rider's hands better than the cheap controls that the de luxe was given in exchange. No-one missed the ratchet stand, a proper propstand being a far better idea, and the suspension, front and rear, was much better then Poppe's design. All that was missed was that indefinable quality 'character'.

The new S8 was felt by many to be the bike that should have been made in the first place. The lighter weight of the bike allied to the thinner wheels and tyres transformed the handling and made the S8 into a pleasant motorcycle. It was still short of power in spite of the sporty throb from the stylish cast-aluminium silencer, but the overall feel of the bike was so much improved that sales were to outstrip the ponderous S7.

After their relatively successful re-launch of the two bikes, BSA completely failed to maintain any momentum on sales or publicity, save for the statutory road tests in the motorcycling press. The sole exception was to take place in 1949.

As a publicity device, a composite S7/S8, JOX 307, was prepared for the sidecar class of the International Six Days Trial. The bike was mostly S7 but with standard wheel-rims to take Trials Universal tyres and higher-compression pistons. Together with a high-level exhaust and sidecar gearing it was hitched to a trials-type sidecar body on a modified BSA chassis.

A later road-test emphasised that the outfit had had a trouble-free run to gain its ISDT 'Gold' but that Achilles' heel of the Sunbeam, the rear drive, had needed to be changed three times in secret, though no mention, understandably, was made of this!

As the Sunbeam slipped quietly into the fifties, with the sportier S8 outselling its portly brother, the experimental shop at Redditch produced other variations on the theme as contenders for production. That none of these made it was probably due to the fat loss which the parent company undoubtedly made on the whole range. Most nearly standard was a 600 cc version of the S7 intended to overcome the onset of the asthma which owners found common among S7s attached to heavy sidecars. The 'beam had always looked like a sidecar puller but in reality was not the world's best at dragging double-adults up steep hills.

Another prototype for the same use was built with a BSA 600 cc four-cylinder engine and a water-cooling radiator under the steering head. The engine had been made to propel a projected rival to Austin's A30, and two cars and two motorcycles were put together. When the costings were done for the car it was found that it could not compete with the A30 and work was stopped. Without the car, the engine would not be available for the Sunbeam and that put paid to the four-cylinder bike. Bits of one of these survive.

The variant that could have done the trick was known as the S10. The worm drive axle was replaced by a hypoid drive as used

Super Profile

by most other shaft-drive bikes. The engine carried forward the S7 de luxe's use of BSA parts by incorporating most of the internals from the 'A' range twin, giving a capacity of 600 cc in a Sunbeam-style crankcase. The motor was of pushrod type with a single, side-mounted camshaft and the styling was that of the S8. Although remembered as an excellent motorcycle, the two prototypes were finally scrapped without compunction as BSA ran further into the difficulties that were to bankrupt the group, and almost no record of them remains.

The S7 de luxe and S8 went on into the mid-fifties with no substantial alterations and no serious attempt to market them. Each year the catalogues were virtually the same; each year the enthusiasts for the make looked in vain for the updating that should have been inevitable, the re-styling and power boost allied to a swinging-arm rear suspension in line with other BSA products. The 'A', 'B' ranges and two-stroke Bantam all got worked on to a greater or lesser degree, but not the Sunbeam.

At last, in 1956, the inevitable happened, and the Sunbeam ceased production. Always a slow seller, even more so than usual when it became obvious that the end was near, the Sunbeam could be found in many dealers' showrooms, at a reduced price, for a couple of years. The name Sunbeam re-appeared a few years later on a short-lived range of scooters.

In Japan, however, all was not dead. The 'fifties were an era in which the Japanese manufacturers were 'borrowing' as many ideas as possible from Western makers. Their oriental products were very derivative, and one of them was based on the S8.

The Liner TW was produced by the Kitagawa Automobile factory at Nakajimacho in Hamamatsu. The firm was established as an independent maker in May 1950 and introduced the Liner TW in 1954. It was the result of the factory's buying three Sunbeams and examining them in detail. The engine was a 360° twin with gear-driven single ohc and produced 126 hp at 5,500 rpm, the bore and stroke being 55 mm x 52 mm and the displacement 250 cc.

There was a significant difference between Japanese and English production, though. In 1955, the Liner was an almost carbon copy of the S8, but by 1957 it had an NSU-style spine frame and swinging-arm suspension at both ends and by 1958 it was out of production as the Liner TW III. The Japanese contempt for yesterday had extracted all the lessons from the Sunbeam and moved on.

In terms of making a profit for BSA the S7 and its derivations were certainly a failure. The early reputation for difficult maintenance and unreliability stuck with the bike and hampered its sales. The spectacle of S7's struggling along with loaded double-adult sidecars did not help the public image and there is no doubt that many motorcyclists looked on the S7 with disgust as being rather 'soft', failing to notice that, as with the S7's BMW ancestors, long distances could be covered without discomfort, in contrast to the pounding taken by the rider on some of the industry's more 'sporting' boneshakers of the day.

The people who took to the Sunbeams were very fond of them and there has remained an enthusiastic following for these idiosyncratic bikes. Most past owners remember them with affection and they never fail to arouse interest when ridden on the road. There is now a club especially for them and this indicates the success of the S7. If only BSA had seen the potential, they might have developed the twins into more of a commercial money-maker and they would then have been a success in both senses.

Machine identification

The frame number is found on the frame lug and the engine number is sited on the right front of the crankcase. The original S7 numbers have an S7 prefix but both S7 de luxe and S8 models made after 1949 have an S8 prefix on the engine, S7 frames retaining an S7 prefix. The engine and frame numbers were normally the same on S7 machines but not so on S7 de luxe and S8 bikes.

The frames of the three models act as a distinctive identification point and the models, although basically similar, cannot easily be confused.

The Sunbeam models used a simple numbering system. Although the original factory records are not now available, the following is a reasonable guide to dating by number. All machines leaving the factory had their date of production on a card sent with the instruction book.

Model S7. First produced from December 21st 1946 with the engine number S7-101 and frame number S7-101. Approximate year numbers are;
1947 Frame from S7-101 to S7-520
1948 Frame from S7-520 to S7-1800
1949 Frame from S7-1800 to S7-2205

10

Super Profile

The last S7 left the factory on April 1st 1949 with engine No. S7-2371 and frame S7-2205.

In 1949, the range was revised to become the S7 de luxe (normally known as the S7, there being no S7 'standard') and the S8. The S7 was invariably finished in 'Sunbeam Mist Green' and the S8 in either black or 'Polychromatic Gun Metal Grey'. After the changeover, all engines bore an S8 prefix, only the frames having an S7 or S8 prefix, according to the model. Model S7 de luxe. First produced from May 27th 1949 with engine number S8 - 462 and frame number S7 - 2501. Subsequently the numbers ran concurrently with those of the S8. As some machines remained 'in stock' at the factory and at dealer's premises for a long time, it is usual to find machines registered much later than the date of manufacture. For example, S8 Frame S8-4663 and Engine S8-7332 left the assembly line on 2nd July 1951. Model S8. First produced from March 25th 1949 with engine number S8-104 and frame number S8-101.

The following numbers apply approximately to the production years.
1949 Frames from S7 - 2501 to S7 - 2900 S8 - 101 to S8 - 1350
1950 Frames from S7 - 2900 to S7 - 4500 S8 - 1350 to S8 - 4500
1951 Frames from S7 - 4500 to S7 - 6000 S8 - 4500 to S8 - 6000
1952 Frames from S7 - 6000 to S7 - 6700 S8 - 6000 to S8 - 6800
1953 Frames from S7 - 6700 to S7 - 7000 S8 - 6800 to S8 - 7400
1954 Frames from S7 - 7000 to S7 - 7500 S8 - 7400 to S8 - 7850
1955 Frames from S7 - 7500 to S7 - 7800 S8 - 7850 to S8 - 8300
1956 Frames from S7 - 7800 on
1956 S8 - 8300 on
Production ceased in 1956

Production Modifications – It should be noted that many of these could be done retrospectively and can not reliably be used for dating.

July 1947. Oil-wick lubrication of the rear suspension discarded in favour of grease-gun lubrication.

September 1947. Ratchet adjustment of kick-start crank angle discarded.

December 1947. Introduction of engine rear top damper, involving lengthened rear engine cover and distributor studs.

July 1948. Heavier rebound spring fitted in rear plunger suspension (Serial 89-4069) to prevent topping of rear suspension over hump-back bridges etc.

July 1948. Revised camshaft (89-379 in place of 89-362) and revised rockers (89-381 in place of 89-362) in order to reduce wear rate. New, lighter valve springs (yellow paint coded) also fitted. Rocker cover needs hand-filing on earlier machines to fit conversion (oil-spray plate area).

September 1948. Weller tensioner deleted in favour of solid-blade, plunger tensioned version standardised on all following Sunbeams. A conversion kit was marketed (Part No. 89-165) for all earlier machines.

September 1948. From Engine S7 - 712 the upper top friction damper plate at the rear of the engine was thickened to prevent fracture.

March 1949. Oil-wick lubrication for the saddle centre-spring deleted in favour of grease-gun operation.

March - May 1949. S7/S8 production resumed after the re-design and re-tooling which resulted in the S7 de luxe and S8.

The S8 frame lacked the cantilever saddle, having mountings instead for a three-point saddle, but was otherwise similar to the S7 de luxe. The rear suspension housing consists of a single metal forging rather than the tube and the lug design of the S7. The engine had new castings with different head and gearbox stud positions and revised mountings, as well as changed oilways and cylinder liner clearances. Old and new are not interchangeable, except as a complete engine/gear unit suitably modified. Rear drive fitted with drain plug.

September 1949. Lucas MC45L dynamo fitted instead of MC45.

February 1950. Changed serial number for the sidecar worm and wheel set – found stamped on wheel edge, visible through inspection plate. Now Worm - 89 - 5536, Wheel 89-5535. Clutch operating lever now non-reversible to take up wear.

March 1950. Oil pressure switch now mounted on an extension to avoid overheating, necessitating a cutaway in the alloy plug cover.

1951-1952. Lucas 477 - 1 stop-tail lamp fitted to both models.

April 1952. Revised timing chain tensioner on all models. Kit (89 - 165) now available for use on S7 prefix engines still fitted with the Weller tensioner.

1952. S7 Models now have two grease nipples to lubricate the cantilever saddle.

1953 - 1956. Lucas 525 stop/tail lamp fitted to all models.

January 1954. Revised crankshaft front bearing utilising a roller bearing instead of a ball-race. Revised crankshaft end-float of 0.004 to 0.007 inch, adjusted by shim.

S7 1946 - 1949

Engine and frame numbers S7 - 101 to S7 - 2900. Engine and

Super Profile

Frame normally carried the same number. Built between 1946 and 1949 at BSA's Redditch factory. The differences in specification between this and the other S7 de luxe and S8 machines are numerous and are indicated where applicable, in the S7 de luxe and S8 specification.

Engine	Air-cooled vertical twin
Capacity	487 cc (29.7 cu in)
Bore	70 mm (2¾ in)
Stroke	63.5 mm (2½ in)
bhp	213 at 5800 rpm
Compression Ratio	6.5:1, 6.8:1, 7.2:1 to choice

Engine block in DTD 424 Alloy fitted with austenitic iron flanged cylinder liners. One-piece two-bearing crankshaft cast in Meehanite GM. Rear main bearing housed in a Meehanite GM casting spigoted into the crankcase. The bearing is a single row ball-race.

The connecting-rods are H-section RR56 forgings with caps held by waisted bolts and lead-bronze bearings with a lead-indium flash.

Pistons are Specialloid, made in SL101C with two pressure rings and one scraper ring.

The cylinder-head is a Y-alloy casting with in-line valves at an angle of 22½ degrees, made from EN54 - V26. The camshaft is in EN32 - V15 and is driven by a single roller chain from a sprocket carried on the crankshaft pinion.

Lubrication is by a gear pump mounted on the main bearing housing driven by gear from the crankshaft pinion. Oil drawn from the sump is passed to an annular space surrounding the main bearing, pressure relieved at 30 psi. From here the oil is carried to the big-end bearings through the hollow crankpins, and through a passage to the camshaft bearings and rocker finger bearings. Other bearings are lubricated by splash and oil mist. The oil returns to the sump via the camshaft chain tunnel.

Transmission

The gearbox case is cast in DTD 424 and is secured to the engine by four studs. The single dry-plate clutch (originally with a rubber cush-drive insert) is operated by a push-rod through the mainshaft from a cable-operated lever. The drive on all gears in indirect, giving ratios of;

1st	3.785 : 1		14.5 : 1
2nd	2.35 : 1	overall	9.0 : 1
3rd	1.68 : 1		6.5 : 1
Top	1.393 : 1		5.3 : 1

All gears are in EN24 - V10 with 12 DP and 20 degree pressure angle. Gearbox shafts are made of EN36 - V18. Gears are selected by a positive-stop mechanism inside the case actuated by right-foot lever. The kickstart mechanism is driven through a right-angle by phosphor-bronze sector to operate the mainshaft and thus the crankshaft. The pedal is thus in the 'normal' position. The drive to the rear 'axle' is by a solid propeller shaft with a flexible coupling at the front end and a Hardy-Spicer universal joint at the back.

The rear drive is a worm and wheel set in a DTD424 housing. The worm is steel and the wheel phosphor-bronze. Drive is taken to the rear wheel by a splined carrier.

Frame

Steel stamped lugs joined by Reynolds 531 or Accles and Pollock chrome molybdenum tubing in a duplex cradle form.

Front fork

Telescopic, with bronze bushes sliding on steel columns held into upper yokes by taper and lower yokes by pinch bolt. Cotton wick is packed into the columns and saturated with oil, which lubricates the column by oil mist spread by the pumping action of the forks.

The springs are contained in a single upper unit linked to each slider by a bridge member and lubricated by grease. There is no damping.

Rear suspension

A tubular central column is located in the frame by pinch bolts and has a slider, with bronze bushes, running upon it. On the offside the endplate of the axle unit is secured to the slider and on the nearside the slider is fitted with a pinch bolt and bracket for the wheel spindle. Above the slider is a 152 lb/in spring and below a lighter rebound spring and laminated rubber stop. The springs are shrouded by metal covers. In early models the same system of wick lubrication as on the front forks is employed; on later ones, grease.

Electrical equipment

All the electrical equipment is of Joseph Lucas manufacture. It is powered by a Lucas MC45 60 watt output crankshaft-driven dynamo, with most of the electrical gear contained in the two boxes under the seat. The offside box houses the ignition switch and ammeter while the nearside one houses the battery. A set of bulb holders for spare bulbs is provided in the box lids.

The eight-inch headlamp contains the Smiths Chronometric speedometer, calibrated to 80 mph, and ignition and oil-pressure warning lights. All electrical controls are integral, the dipswitch being in the form of a left-hand twistgrip with built-in horn button.

S7 de luxe 1949 - 1956

The general layout is very similar to that of the S7 model, with the major modifications not affecting the overall appearance.

The engine block, head and sump castings are new, though of similar design to the S7. The main changes are to the frame and forks, electrical equipment remaining almost as on the S7.

Front suspension

The front forks are of the same basic design as fitted to many BSA models of the period. The fork yokes are wide to accommodate the 4.50/4.75-16 tyres. Each leg contains a reservoir of oil which is used in a progressive hydraulic damping system giving greater resistance towards the end of the fork stroke. Each leg contains a long, helical spring, all moving parts being covered by metal shrouds styled after those on the original S7.

Rear suspension

Again, the basic design of the rear suspension follows that of BSA models of the period. The principle is the same as that of the original S7 but dimensions differ and there is grease-gun lubrication.

S8 1949 - 1956

The differences between the S7 de luxe and S8 may be summarised, as follows:

	S7	S8
Silencer	Absorption type Chromium plated	Baffle type, cast aluminium
Wheels	Detachable and interchangeable, enamel finish	Detachable, chrome finish
Tyres	Front: 4.50-16 ribbed Rear: 4.75-16 studded	Front: 3.25-19 ribbed Rear: 4.00-18 studded
Brakes	8 in diameter, Sunbeam design	Front: 7 in diameter BSA Rear: 8 in diameter. Sunbeam design
Saddle	Spring cradle cantilever adjustable for rider's weight	Three-point attachment
Finish	Mist green enamel with black frame and chrome-plated fittings	Black or silver-grey enamel with black frame and chrome-plated fittings.

Super Profile

Performance

	S7	S8
Maximum bhp at rpm	25 - 5800	25 - 5800
Maximum speed (solo) mph	75 - 80	80 - 85
kph	120 - 128	128 - 136
Maximum speed (sidecar) mph	55 - 60	60 - 65
kph	88 - 96	96 - 104
Petrol consumption (solo) mpg	70 - 75	70 - 75
l/100 km	3.9	3.9
Petrol consumption (sidecar) mpg	60 - 65	60 - 65
l/100 km	4.5	4.5

Dimensions

	S7	S8
Wheelbase (in)	57	57
(cm)	144	144
Ground clearance (in)	$4\frac{1}{2}$	$5\frac{1}{2}$
(cm)	11	14
Saddle height (in)	$30\frac{1}{2}$	30
(cm)	$77\frac{1}{2}$	76
Width (in)	31	31
(cm)	79	79
Length (in)	86	86
(cm)	218	218
Height (in)	$40\frac{1}{4}$	$40\frac{1}{4}$
(cm)	102	102
Dry weight (lb)	430	405
(kg)	196	184

Super Profile

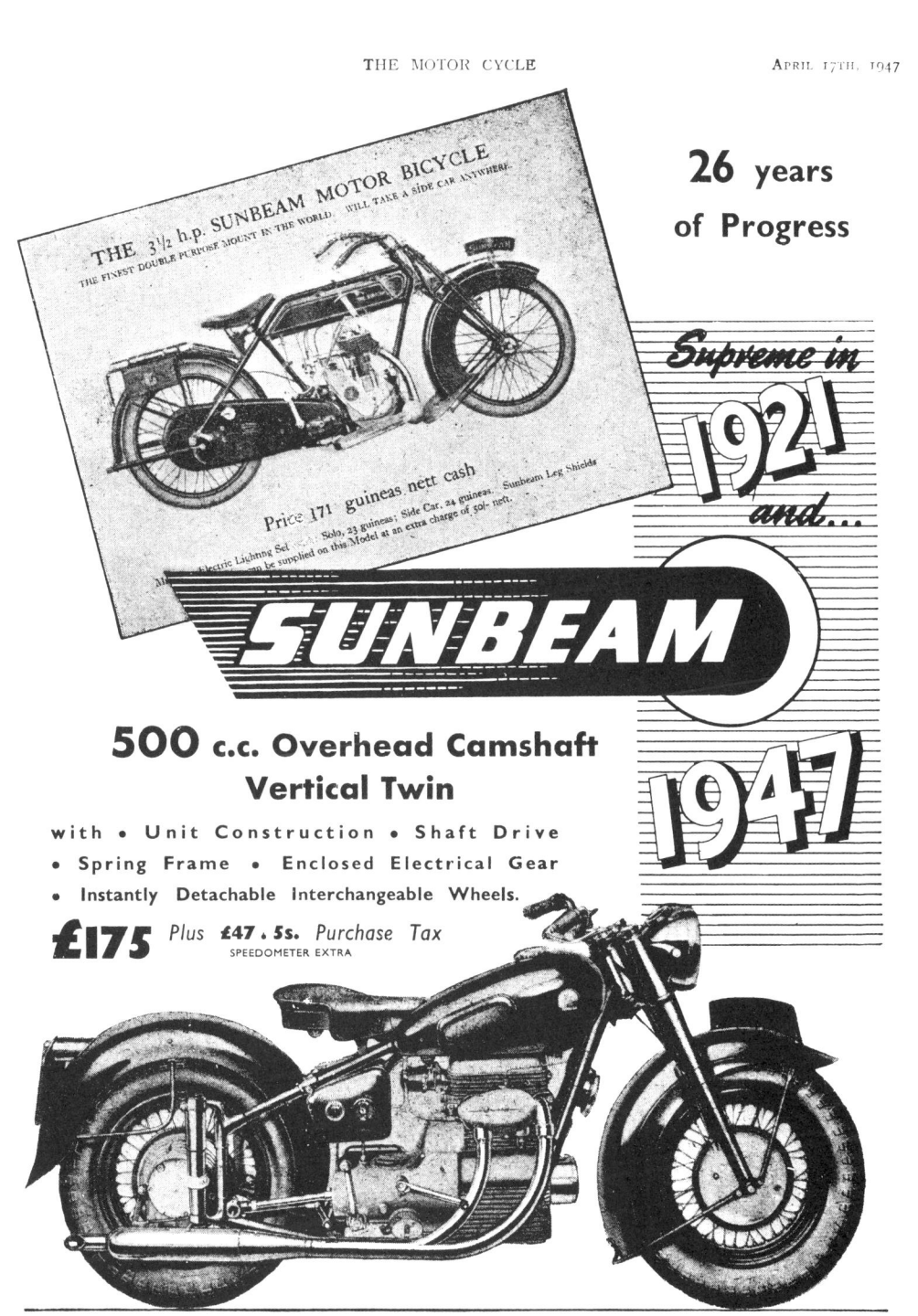

THE MOTOR CYCLE   APRIL 17TH, 1947

26 years of Progress

THE 3½ h.p. SUNBEAM MOTOR BICYCLE
THE FINEST DOUBLE PURPOSE MOUNT IN THE WORLD. WILL TAKE A SIDE CAR ANYWHERE.

Price 171 guineas nett cash
Solo, 23 guineas; Side Car, 24 guineas. Sunbeam Leg Shields
can be supplied on this Model at an extra charge of 50/- nett.

Supreme in **1921** *and...* **1947**

SUNBEAM

500 c.c. Overhead Camshaft Vertical Twin

with • Unit Construction • Shaft Drive
• Spring Frame • Enclosed Electrical Gear
• Instantly Detachable Interchangeable Wheels.

£175 Plus **£47.5s.** Purchase Tax
SPEEDOMETER EXTRA

SUNBEAM CYCLES LTD., BIRMINGHAM, 11.

Super Profile

ROAD TESTS

CHARLES MARKHAM Samples

and ROAD TESTS the
VERTICAL

Facts about the Performance of a Shaft-driven, Rear-sprung Machine which Forms One of the Most Sensational Post War Designs

(Above) An outstanding feature of this remarkable mount is the little demand it makes of its pilot when covering long distances at high speed. (Right) A close look at "The New Look." Notable are the streamlined plug-shield, the battery-case and accessible oil-filler-cum-dipstick in the crankcase.

WHEN informed that the latest edition of Sunbeam Model S7 was awaiting test, I ventured to express the idea that a mere 1,000 miles would do little more than perform an introduction; with a machine so revolutionary, it might be necessary to overcome the reluctancy of conventional thought, etc. In the course of many road tests one learns a notable fact, i.e., that first reactions are unreliable factors when set against final assessment. The 'Beam provided an outstanding example of this necessity to overcome preconceived notions by reason of its highly individual " soling and heeling." Tyre sections measuring 4.50 ins. by 16 ins. front and 4.75 ins. by 16 ins. rear looked all against the set principles of good handling; but three miles after our first meeting I was riding along a wet tramline at 25 m.p.h. and whistling, " Begone, dull care!"

Mechanical silence was almost unbelievable, and it hardly seems possible that any air-cooled unit will ever surpass the standard set by this motor. Come to a temporary halt in traffic, shut the grip, and it is literally impossible for an onlooker more than ten yards away to detect whether the engine is running or not.

Starting was child's play, and just to prove the point, I can tell you that an average young lady of 12 years set the unit in motion with a single prod—and then repeated the performance *by hand*—this with the engine barely warm! From dead cold it was necessary only to administer two sucking-in strokes with the carburetter bell-type strangler closed, switch on, and the next dig would produce a tick-over so slow that every single beat could be counted.

Rubber engine mounting is yet a novelty to most motor-cyclists, and I never got tired of displaying the fascinating wobble so boldly evident at tick-over revolutions, whilst the curious " remoteness " at normal road speeds imparted a constant impression of free-wheeling. There was, however, a distinct " period " at 26-28 m.p.h. in top and corresponding speeds in the lower gears. Flexible handle-bar mounting and foot-rest rubbers so expansive that you could " go for a walk on 'em " all added to the impression of luxurious travel With its spring unit sliding in the frame top tube and adjustment provided for riders of varying weights, the special Terry saddle gives first-class

Super Profile

"THE NEW LOOK"
487c.c. o.h.c. Model S7
TWIN SUNBEAM

travel devoid of lateral sway or sudden shocks. Plunger rear-springing of the "soft" variety, with 3½-in. total movement, helps to put the whole of the rear-end suspension into the limousine class.

Would that I could pay such glowing praise to the front-fork suspension, which is reasonable without approaching the high standard of the hindquarters. Rightly or wrongly, I gained the impression that a softer springing would help to cut out the suggestion that bumps and undulations were present. In these days of sensitive "telescopics" we are used to seeing cross-gullies vanish beneath without visible lift occurring at the top fork bridge. From 63 m.p.h. upwards, the Sunbeam's front wheel began to hop in a most disconcerting manner, but I could remove both hands from the bars at 70 m.p.h. and still follow my-nose in the approved fashion. Any idea that this might be a common fault was shaken by a chat with a private owner who simply appeared puzzled when I hinted at the point.

Those timid souls who look upon motorcycle controls with the same awestruck mental fog reserved for the odd glimpse of a Lancaster's cockpit, could scarcely cavil at the 'Beam. Twist-grips control throttle and dip light; the horn button is built-in on the left-hand grip, whilst clutch and front brake are operated by inverted levers—and I *didn't* find these latter controls awkward or difficult in use! More "bite" on the front stopper would be a great advantage, for the S7 is no lightweight.

The twist-grip dipper action is good, neat and it is conveniently placed, but my particular sample possessed an unwelcome neutral. I hit a series of severe ripples one night, hung grimly on to the bars and unconsciously turned the grip—whereupon somebody seemed to put a "black" penny in the meter and a slight panic set in!

High-speed braking on the rear only produced a faint judder, but definitely no cause for alarm, and the 4.75-in. by 16-in. tyre clung to the road with the persistency of jam on flannel suiting. The clutch is beautifully responsive and as smooth as velvet, whilst it would be difficult indeed to instance a lighter gear change. You merely take a little

(Left) Rubber engine mountings are an unusual detail of the design. Here is the cushioned-top forward damping member

(Below) Modernity in motorcycles. The model S7 Sunbeam creates a stir wherever it is seen—and you will learn why from this account of its characteristics.

Without hurrying, this youngster keeps pace easily with the Sunbeam, while rider Markham, his hand well away from the clutch, lets it tick along in low gear.

care on timing, and the ratio is swapped with consummate ease. Silent drive on all gears ensures that the intermediates can be usefully employed without orchestral accompaniment, wear or fuss. Apart from a distinctive exhaust note, the only audible evidence of progress at any speed was a faint whine from the transmission, heard only when the ear was turned away from wind roar.

Mounted in the head-lamp shell and set at just the right angle for ready visibility, the speedometer is ideally situated. It is flanked on either side by tell-tale lights—red for ignition, green for oil—and the latter refuses to be forgotten. Just as soon as the sump level requires 1-pt. replenishment it begins an intermittent winking, which I found so irritating that it was a pleasure to pause and top-up. Oil consumption averaged 380 miles to the pint, and a dipstick is incorporated in the filler cap situated on the near side of the crankcase. Not once in 2,700 miles was the engine exterior

338 MOTOR CYCLING March 4, 1948.

BRIEF SPECIFICATION OF 487 c.c. o.h.c. MODEL S7 SUNBEAM TWIN

Engine: Vertical in-line twin; bore 70 mm. and stroke 64 mm.=487 c.c.; chain-driven overhead camshaft with valves set in single row; squish-type heads with 6.2-to-1 compression ratio; one-piece aluminium-alloy cylinder head; one-piece crankcase and cylinder-block casting with Austenitic cylinder liners; light-alloy connecting rods with lead-bronze big-ends; wet-sump lubrication with oil carried in cast-aluminium sump bolted to lower face of crankcase, capacity 3 pints; gear-type oil pump located in rear-bearing housing and driven from crankshaft; coil ignition with automatic advance and Lucas 40-watt dynamo driven from front of crankshaft; Amal carburetter with air-bell strangler control.

Transmission: Gearbox in unit with engine; built-in positive-stop gear change; ratios 5.31, 6.48, 9.02 and 14.5 to 1; single-plate clutch; final drive by shaft and underslung worm.

Frame: Heavy-gauge duplex loop type with plunger rear suspension and helical springs; telescopic front forks with springs enclosed in centre tube; bolted-up front stand; ratchet-controlled centre stand.

Wheels: Fitted with Dunlop tyres, 4.50 by 16-in. front ribbed and 4.75 by 16-in. rear Universal; fulcrum-pin adjustment to front and rear brakes.

Tank: Welded-steel fuel tank, 3¼-gallon capacity, with built-in knee-grips.

Dimensions: Saddle height, 28½ ins.; wheelbase, 56 ins.; ground clearance, 5½ ins.; overall width, 33 ins.; weight (with 1 gallon of fuel), 411 lb.

Finish: High-quality black with chromium exhaust system leading into common silencer; chromium-plated fittings.

Equipment: Lucas lighting with 8-in. head lamp and "flat-beam" fluted front; twist-grip dip control; electric horn; speedometer built into head lamp; warning ignition and oil light in head-lamp shell.

Price: £175, plus £47 5s. purchase tax, total £222 5s. Speedometer £4 extra, plus £1 1s. 8d. p.t.

Makers: Sunbeam Cycles, Ltd., Birmingham, 11.

cleaned, and not a single oil leak was visible after this mileage.

In studying performance figures it is as well to remember that this model S7 does not pretend to offer rocketing get-away or super-sporting maximum. What it does in terms of maximum m.p.h. matters not so much as an undoubted facility for putting many restful road miles into each hour of cross-country travel. A 78-mile run on a busy trunk route was regularly accomplished in an hour and 40 minutes, and a 140-mile non-stop gallop northwards from Birmingham was reeled off in three hours and a quarter. Cruising speed lay anywhere between 58-65 m.p.h., and if acceleration was required below 45 m.p.h. I made a regular habit of dropping into third, and holding it until the "clock" announced a full 60 "per." If the unit objected to this kind of treatment it failed to show it, and the only bother I ever suffered was a sooty rear plug following a long day in Birmingham traffic. It seemed well-nigh impossible to "tire" the engine.

Wide Speed Range

This Sunbeam will quite happily whisper along with 8-9 m.p.h. on the "clock" and with top gear engaged—yet will open up from this crawl without a solitary "pink." In bottom gear, with the throttle closed, I found it easy to put the bars on full lock and turn circles without touching the clutch or even laying a finger on the left bar. Despite the weight it would travel in a dead-straight line at a 3 m.p.h. walking speed.

A ratchet retainer, with a quick-release, foot-operated lever, prevents the machine rolling off its central stand and thereby messing-up that "New Look," but I did object to gripping a muddy rear guard-stay in order to park in the approved manner. Speaking of mudguarding, I cheerfully undertook city trips without leg protection despite showery conditions and damp surfaces. At the close of one wintry week, during which 600 very wet miles had been recorded, I decided that a wash and brush-up was needed to restore that pristine brilliance. Mrs. M. handed me a bucket of warm water (note the luxury) with a warning that lunch was due half an hour later. With five full minutes to spare the 'Beam was back under cover, washed, dried and polished. Bless those smooth exteriors and easy-clean wheels—and the absence of external oil! I didn't clean the engine or bevel housing because I wanted to observe possible leakages.

Fuel Consumption

Looking over the test sheet you will notice that fuel consumption is actually better on town work than on open roads. Nearly 80 m.p.g. could be obtained by gentle running, but 45 m.p.h. averages would reduce the figure to 55-60 m.p.g. By using one petrol tap only, it was possible to trap sufficient fuel in the tank for a five-mile reserve when its opposite number was switched on. No actual reserve tap is fitted.

Despite frequent and hard use throughout the test, neither brake required adjustment—which is effected by turning a squared fulcrum pin. I suffered some slight bother with a sticking throttle slide which obligingly cured itself, and the toolbox, located on the near side below the battery case, was never "opened in anger."

A few turns with a coin in the slot of a retaining screw opens up the battery casing and reveals the neat rubber buffer mounting. The same easy method on the off-side located switchbox housing and there, "before your very eyes," is the lighting switch and ammeter wiring neatly located in the lid. Inside the case are the voltage regulator unit and ignition coil. Really quickly detachable and interchangeable wheels are hereby noted and duly appreciated.

The bogy known as "torque reaction" was present in such slight degree that it may be brushed off without further ado. It could be felt only when blipping the throttle from the slowest tickover.

Withal, I look upon that month with the "New Look" as a very pleasant memory. Here is a machine which fulfils almost every expressed ideal of the motorcyclist who desires luxurious transport for daily or week-end travel. No question of a get-away like a bank robbery, but swift and silent progress to fit the varying mood of the tourist—the man who forms the backbone of our pastime.

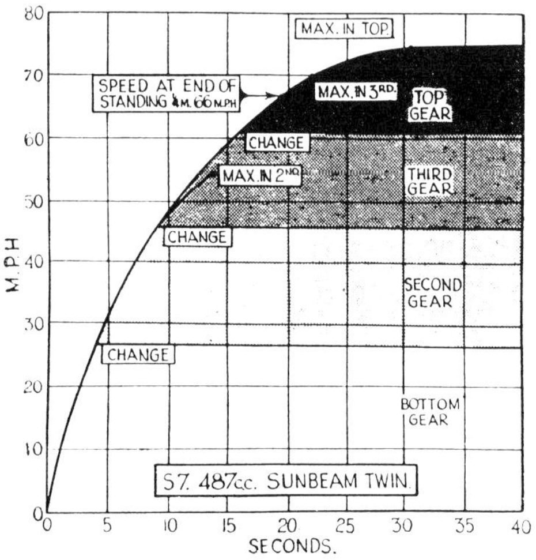

MOTOR CYCLING

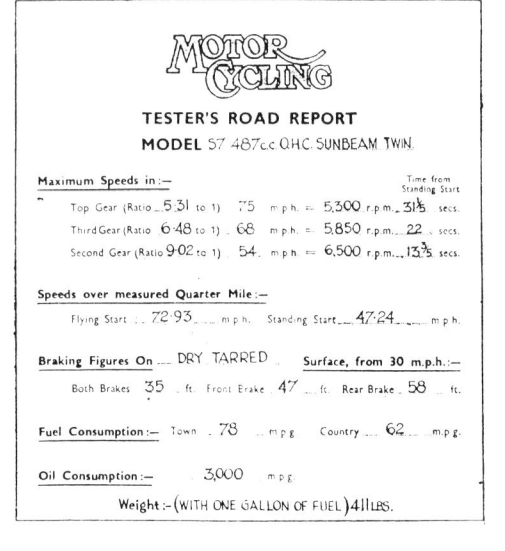

TESTER'S ROAD REPORT

MODEL S7 487c.c. O.H.C. SUNBEAM TWIN.

Maximum Speeds in:— (Time from Standing Start)

Top Gear (Ratio 5·31 to 1) 75 m.p.h. = 5,300 r.p.m. 31⅕ secs.

Third Gear (Ratio 6·48 to 1) 68 m.p.h. = 5,850 r.p.m. 22 secs.

Second Gear (Ratio 9·02 to 1) 54 m.p.h. = 6,500 r.p.m. 13⅗ secs.

Speeds over measured Quarter Mile:—

Flying Start 72·93 m.p.h. Standing Start 47·24 m.p.h.

Braking Figures On DRY TARRED **Surface, from 30 m.p.h.:—**

Both Brakes 35 ft. Front Brake 47 ft. Rear Brake 58 ft.

Fuel Consumption:— Town 78 m.p.g. Country 62 m.p.g.

Oil Consumption:— 3,000 m.p.g.

Weight:— (WITH ONE GALLON OF FUEL) 411 LBS.

Super Profile

ROAD TESTS OF CURRENT MODELS—

THE 487 c.c. MODEL S8 o.h.c. VERTICAL TWIN
SUNBEAM

PROBABLY no post-war motorcycles have aroused more interest than the "S" series of Sunbeams, the first description of which appeared in "Motor Cycling's" issue of March 7, 1946, followed by a road test of a production model S7 published on March 4, 1948.

The S8, the second model of the series, developed from the S7, perpetuates now well-established Sunbeam tradition. The design in its entirety caters for the modern school of thought which, without wholly disregarding the healthy spirit inseparable from an essentially sporting mode of transport, does, to-day, underline rather heavily such very desirable and practical aspects as comfort, freedom from undue noise, unnecessary dirt and tinkering.

Three freedoms, as it were, and of them the last-mentioned is probably uppermost not only in the minds of "Motor Cycling" staffmen who have recently shared some 900 enjoyable miles on a 1950 S8 Sunbeam, but also in those of customers—lucky men—who, particularly in the dollar countries, think in terms of harder riding and longer mileages than are contemplated by the average Britisher. The latter, of course, is handicapped by petrol rationing for one thing but, too, he simply has not thousands of miles of country available in these Isles for prolonged bouts of riding.

Conceivably many, who are possibly seeing the S8 for the first time at the British Show in New York, are thinking of it in terms of 500-mile runs; town-to-town distances in the United States, and other parts of the world, cultivate that line of thought. It is opportune to mention, therefore, that at one phase of "Motor Cycling's" test, Midland-man Dennis Hardwicke covered just this distance in less than 24 hours. And he finished fresh, enthusiastic about the relatively high cruising speed possible and, more important, the sheer impossibility of fatiguing the 487 c.c. o.h.c. in-line twin-cylinder engine.

Other staff members who rode the model extolled its readiness to give day-in and day-out service without necessary recourse to the toolbox, or apprehension on the part of the rider about Sunbeam reliability, even though coil

The Sports Version of a Unique Shaft-drive Machine Which Gave a New Look to British Motorcycle Design

Well-known race rider Phil Heath, who collaborated with "Motor Cycling" in this test, finds out how the 'Beam handles at speed.

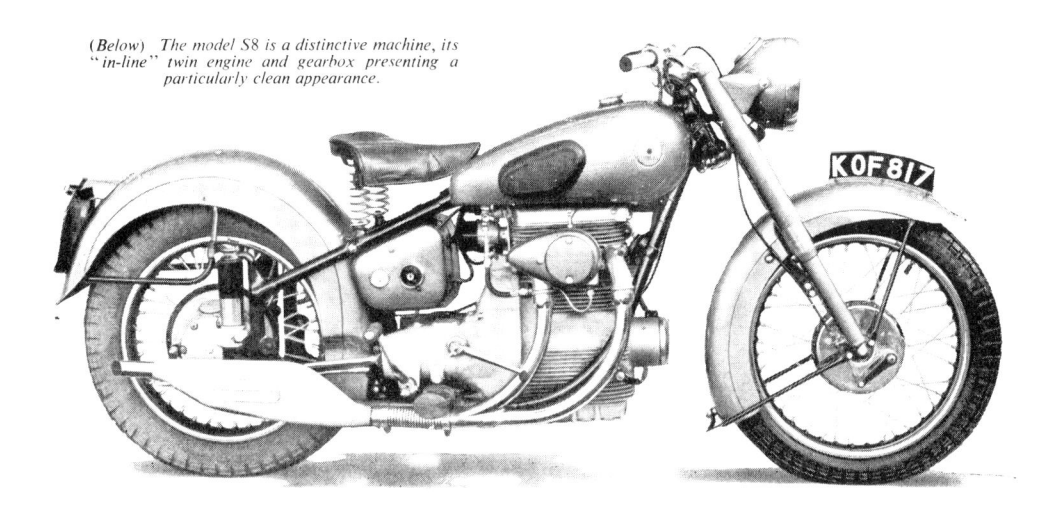

(Below) The model S8 is a distinctive machine, its "in-line" twin engine and gearbox presenting a particularly clean appearance.

Super Profile

ignition, and not a magneto, is favoured by its manufacturer.

The designer has shown bold wisdom over this matter, for there is no gainsaying that first-kick starting is more likely to be assured by the fat spark from a battery than from low-tension current generated initially by a magneto armature rotating at low r.p.m. Nor throughout the speed range of the S8, the top end of which touches the 80 m.p.h. mark, is there any suggestion of voltage drop.

For years motorcyclists have said: "Give us car-type coil ignition." Sunbeam's have done more; they have avoided the conventional, clipped-on coil by enclosing it, together with the ammeter and compensated voltage control unit in an unobtrusive box blending well with the general lines of the machine.

Externally the box carries the ammeter and switchgear, which means that, whilst the complete Sunbeam wiring loom is perhaps a little more complicated than is normally accepted layout, bunches of cables running between widely spaced components are avoided.

One of Hardwicke's colleagues voiced the criticism that, in manipulating the switch and ignition key, he had to fumble instead of being able to move his hand from the bars to the more usual head-lamp switch mounting. It is

(Above) The nearside of the o.h.c. engine. Note the streamlined, finned plug protector, the oil filler, and the 60w. crankshaft-driven Lucas dynamo. (Below) The electric control mechanism is well protected and readily accessible.

The Sunbeam's silence and comfort make long distance riding effortless so far as the pilot is concerned.

a valid viewpoint; on the other hand, usage and the familiarity which comes with ownership as opposed to temporary test riding, would soon mould a new habit.

With the ignition switched on a conventional, red tell-tale lamp, situated in the head-lamp shell, lights up. A second circuit embodies a green warning light. With the fuel turned on and after very slight depression of the Amal float-chamber "tickler," a single, almost lazy dab on the kick-starter suffices to bring the power unit to life, at which juncture both the warning lights go out. At anything above walking pace in bottom gear—and you can really get down to a 4 m.p.h. gait without difficulty—they stay out unless the sump oil level drops, in which case the green tell-tale winks urgently and brightly and continues to do so until the rider stops and does a little topping up. Oddly, it's not a thing you can ignore, promising yourself that if the oil *is* a little low it'll be all right until you get home. The little light is annoyingly efficient!

The Sunbeam engine is free to move independently of its frame, so absorbing its own torque reaction. Actually, the S8 unit is suspended by bonded-rubber mountings, the whole of the lower part being free literally to "wobble" sideways within limits defined by rubber buffers. Thus, so soon as the throttle is blipped slightly, producing a rise in r.p.m. equal to, say, 4-10 m.p.h. in bottom gear, the resulting torque reaction, instead of being transferred to the machine and possibly upsetting low-speed steering, quickly spends itself. Apart from a slight quiver noticeable chiefly if the throttle is intentionally tweaked open, vibration is completely absent.

From bottom to second gear and then to the third ratio, a little practice is necessary before the right technique with the positive-stop foot-change mechanism is acquired. This, probably, is accounted for by reason of the clutch running at engine speed; judging the correct moment for changing and then moving the lever with a slight "dwell," is an art soon learnt. And when the rider has mastered it, exceptionally easy and perfectly silent changes are possible.

Between third and top, whether changing up or down, "swopping the cogs" was simplicity itself either at high or low speeds. It was found perfectly satisfactory to take the

BRIEF SPECIFICATION OF THE 487 c.c. o.h.c. MODEL S8 SUNBEAM TWIN

Engine: Vertical in-line twin; bore 70 mm. and stroke 64 mm. = 487 c.c.; chain-driven overhead camshaft with valves set in single row; squish-type heads with 7.2 to 1 compression ratio; one-piece aluminium-alloy cylinder head; one-piece crankcase and cylinder block casting with Austenitic steel cylinder liners; light-alloy connecting rods with lead-bronze big-ends; wet-sump lubrication with oil carried in cast-aluminium sump bolted to lower face of crank-case, capacity 3 pints; gear-type oil pump located in rear-bearing housing and driven from crankshaft; coil ignition with automatic advance and Lucas 60-watt dynamo driven from front of crankshaft; Amal carburetter with strangler control.

Transmission: Gearbox in unit with engine; built-in positive-stop gear change; ratios 5.3, 6.5, 9.00 and 14.5 to 1; single-plate clutch; final drive by shaft and underslung worm.

Frame: Heavy-gauge duplex loop type with plunger rear suspension and helical springs; hydraulic controlled telescopic front forks; bolted-up front stand; centre stand.

Wheels: Fitted with Dunlop Universal tyres, 3.25 by 19-in. front and 4.00 by 18-in. rear; fulcrum-pin adjustment to 7-in. front and 8-in. rear brakes.

Tank: Welded-steel fuel tank, 3½-gallon capacity, with built-in knee-grips.

Dimensions: Saddle height, 30 ins.; wheelbase, 57 ins.; ground clearance, 5½ ins.; overall width, 33 ins.; weight, 420 lb.

Finish: As standard, black with chromium exhaust system leading into common silencer; chromium-plated fittings. Polychromatic grey, as tested, extra.

Equipment: Lucas lighting with 8-in. head lamp and "flat-beam" fluted front; twist-grip dip control; electric horn; speedometer built into head lamp; warning ignition and oil light in head-lamp shell.

Makers: Sunbeam Cycles, Ltd., Birmingham, 11.

---

engine up to its maximum of nearly 6,000 r.p.m. in "third," shut off slightly, declutch and slip into "top." That process, or the opposite one, was described by all who rode the 'Beam in the single word—delightful.

High speeds have been mentioned. In truth it was never the aim of the Sunbeam concern to base their design primarily upon the needs of fast performance. For those who, in 1948, did not have the opportunity of seeing the S7 test figures, let it be said that this engine, with a 6.8-to-1 compression ratio, put out 25 b.h.p., which produced a maximum road speed of 75 m.p.h. In the S8 the c.r. has been stepped up to 7.2, bringing the usable maximum to 80 m.p.h.

80 m.p.h. in 40 secs.

The writer once obtained a flash speed of 85 m.p.h. between Birmingham and London. On the other hand, "80" was attainable in something like 40 secs. from a standing start at any time.

During fairly harsh acceleration a suspicion of pinking occurred in second and third gears; the reason, doubtless, was the comparatively high c.r. plus the quality of British "Pool."

Export buyers, with their higher octane fuel, probably are not troubled with detonation and, moreover, are able to get the needle around the Smiths speedometer towards that "85" mark with far greater regularity than is possible over here just at present.

So much for performance. What about that comfort factor? On the S8 the special Sunbeam forks and Terry saddle used for the early series have been replaced by "teles." of a more conventional type and a normal three-point saddle supported on long coil springs. Rear plunger-type springing is standard and the whole combines to give a very comfortable ride even over very long distances.

Main road surface irregularities—sunken manhole covers and the like—pass beneath the machine unnoticed even though the big 4.50-in. by 16-in. tyres of the S7, too, have been superseded. The S8 carries 3.25-in. by 19-in. front and 4.00-in. by 18-in. rear tyres. Both wheels are instantly detachable.

Whilst it may not matter so much to overseas buyers, whose petrol is unrationed, the home market may voice criticism of the fuel figures recorded whilst the S8 was in our hands. Few owners, for instance, will feel disposed to cruise at 30 m.p.h. to obtain 80 m.p.g. With silky smoothness, speeds very readily soar to the 50 m.p.h. mark where just a little less than 70 m.p.g. can be anticipated—by test standards. Those standards are necessarily harsh, of course. Moreover, a model used by several people is seldom anywhere near so economical as one ridden and cared for by a single owner.

Are there any other queries? Yes, the brakes might be just a *little* more positive. Or was it just a shortcoming of our particular test model? The linings were certainly well bedded down, yet repeated efforts failed to better the 33-ft. stopping distance shown on the Road Report. Weight? A trifle high, perhaps, although there was never any question of the model feeling unwieldy.

Not a very formidable array of criticism, is it? What about some other *good* points? There's the new polychromatic grey finish which definitely doesn't show the dirt. Or the baffle-type cast aluminium silencer which, without detracting from performance, enables you to whisper through a village at dead of night. The Lucas 8-in. head lamp adequately lights your way on such journeys, and, of course, there is that smooth, silent and spotlessly clean shaft drive.

But perhaps the best testimony of all is the confession that at least three fairly hardened members of "Motor Cycling's" staff were genuinely sorry when the time came for this excellent machine to be returned to the works. It had given us some of our most pleasant motorcycling experienced since post-war road-tests were started.

MOTOR CYCLING

TESTER'S ROAD REPORT

MODEL SUNBEAM 500 O.H.C. S8

Maximum Speeds in :—

			Time from Standing Start
Top Gear (Ratio 5.3 to 1)	80 m.p.h.	5399 r.p.m.	40 secs.
Third Gear (Ratio 6.5 to 1)	72 m.p.h.	5976 r.p.m.	22⅖ secs.
Second Gear (Ratio 9.0 to 1)	58 m.p.h.	6665 r.p.m.	12⅘ secs.

Speeds over measured Quarter Mile :—

Flying Start ..... 75.0 m.p.h.   Standing Start ..... 48.9 m.p.h.

Braking Figures On ..... TARRED ..... Surface, from 30 m.p.h. :—

Both Brakes 33 ft.   Front Brake 59 ft.   Rear Brake 52 ft.

Fuel Consumption :— 30 m.p.h. 80 m.p.g. 50 m.p.h. 69 m.p.g. 70 m.p.h. 45 m.p.g.

Oil Consumption :— NEGLIGIBLE m.p.g.

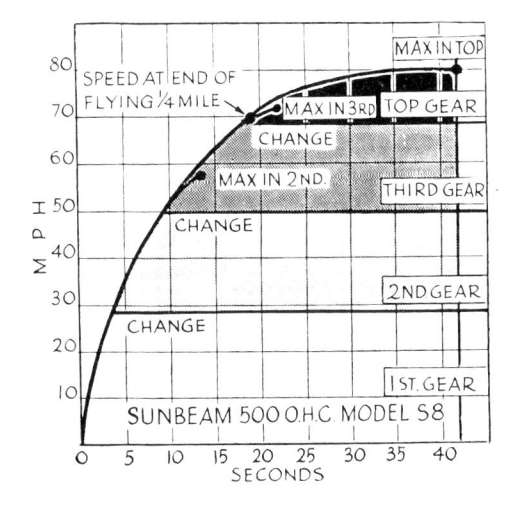

Super Profile

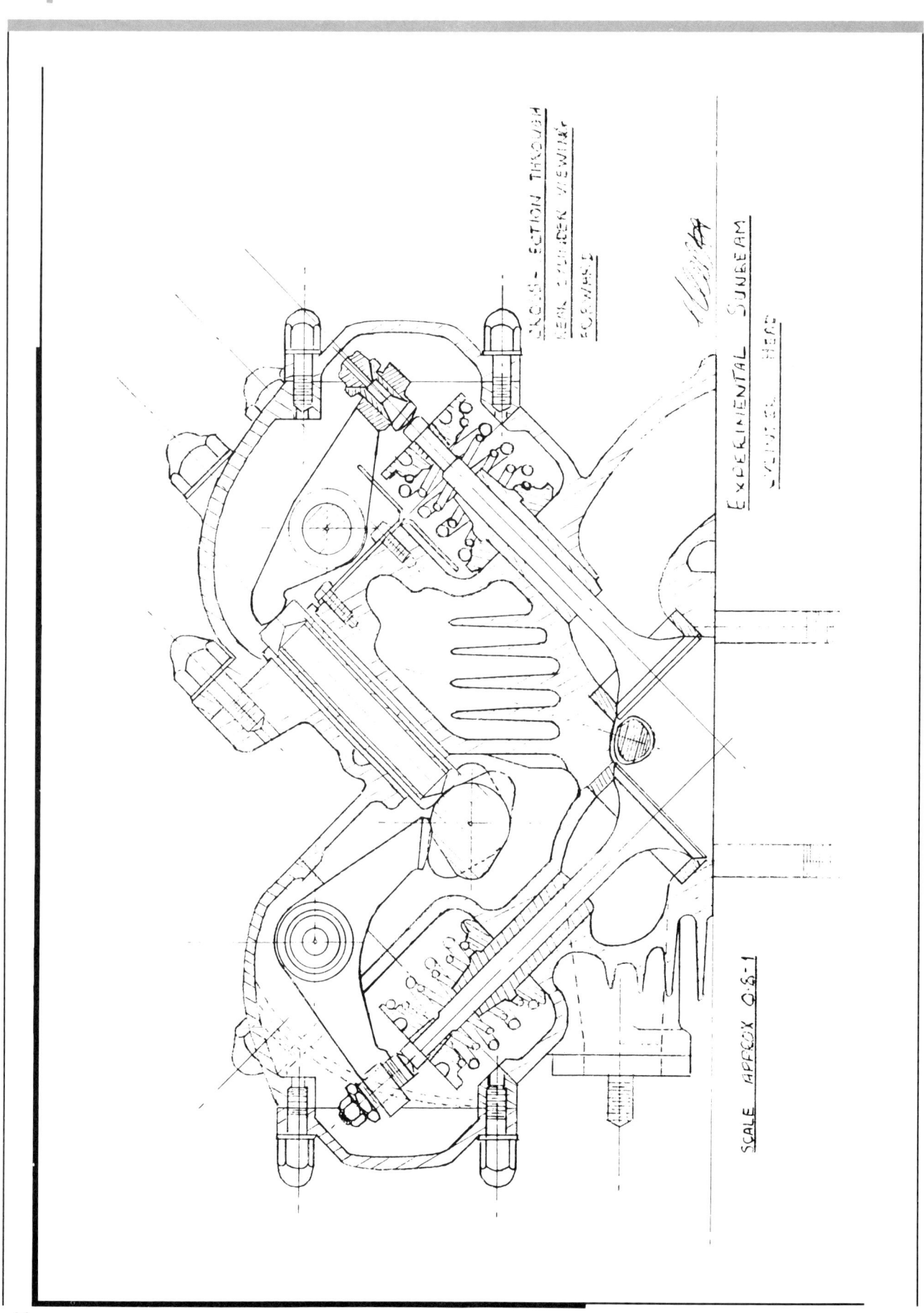

Super Profile

OWNER'S VIEW

The author's first interview was with Peter Ashen, an S8 owner and Sunbeam enthusiast.

RCC: Why are you so interested in the S8?
PA: I bought it to complete my riding experience of Sunbeams, having a 1925 Model 7 and a 1931 Model 90 already, riding them extensively.
RCC: When did you buy your S8 RHA 432?
PA: 1975.
RCC: In what condition was the bike?
PA: A dismantled non-runner with many parts missing. I imagined that a bike in this condition, properly rebuilt, would provide a better buy than a machine which had been rebuilt by someone else whose standards may not have been the same as my own.
RCC: What repair and renovation has been done?
PA: Obviously a complete paint and chrome replacement, to a reasonably high standard. The engine was given new bearings throughout and pistons. The clutch was replaced, as was the bronze wheel in the rear drive. I fitted alloy rims because their appearance complemented that of the matt alloy of the engine unit, giving more of a sense of style than the chromium plated ones. After riding a standard S8 I also replaced the front brake with the BSA Gold Star type unit which gives far superior braking when properly bedded in. This conversion involves no modification whatsoever to the S8 and I have kept the original brake in case I feel suicidal! The tank badge is now black and gold, rather than blue, for tradition's sake!
RCC: Have you experienced difficulty in obtaining spares?
PA: Not at all. All the spares I required were easily and swiftly found. They can cost a lot, though.
RCC: What kind of performance and handling does the Sunbeam have?
PA: The Sunbeam is not a machine that fulfils one's initial expectations and at first seems very disappointing. A long period of learning is needed because the S8 will not change – the owner has to get used to the Sunbeam's peculiarities and adapt his riding style to suit. The Sunbeam is rather short of power and the gear ratios are not well chosen. This impedes progress in hilly country or on twisting roads. The ideal riding medium is a flattish, open road and on this the bike is very pleasant. It is an excellent bike for the nature or scenery lover as its leisurely progress allows time for looking around! As the owner sets up the bike more and more accurately to suit his riding style the irritations disappear. The roadholding is good at normal speeds except in high winds, which can lead to a lot of 'tacking' in order to keep a fairly straight course. The kneegrips are vital and their use aids stability to a great degree. It is very comfortable.
RCC: What sort of use does your Sunbeam get?
PA: The S8 is in more or less regular use for local trips of twenty miles or so. It is also used for medium-distance touring, including holidays, when beween two and four hundred miles may be covered with ease and with no discomfort at all.
RCC: Has your machine won any prizes in concours or similar events?
PA: I have only entered it in one such event, a Vintage Motor Cycle Club Saundersfoot Rally, and it won its class in the concours.
RCC: Do you enter it in any form of motorsport?
PA: Only in VMCC club social runs – I use my vintage Sunbeams for the main events in the club.
RCC: Have you found the Owners' Fellowship to be helpful?
PA: I have not become a member.
RCC: Are there specialists whom you have found helpful?
PA: Yes. Stewart Engineering have, up to now, been most helpful with parts and publications and most of my technical advice has come from you.
RCC: How would you sum up the enjoyment you get from your S8?
PA: Most of the enjoyment has come, and still does, from the steady improvement in our relationship caused by my learning to ride the S8, and taking time to eradicate the problems left after the rebuild. The S8 was 'run-in' over a three-thousand mile period, very carefully, and the effort was well worth it. As one grows used to the machine one ceases to be worried at its foibles – the excessive heat coming through the casings of the dynamo and the reardrive for instance, and enjoys the ride more. One run to Banbury over clear open roads early on a fine, warm day provided me with my most enjoyable motorcycle ride ever. The comfort and electric motor smoothness enabled me to enjoy the day and the countryside and the roads were the type that the Sunbeam enjoys best. Wonderful.
RCC: What advice would you give to prospective purchasers?
PA: It is important to study other owners' comments and to listen to what they say before deciding to buy a Sunbeam. Evaluate whether the 'gentle' nature of the bike will suit your temperament – I am lucky enough to have a Model 90 Sunbeam to use if I feel like going fast.

If most of the riding is done alone, then the S8 is enjoyable, but its speeds and gear ratios do not make riding in company with

Super Profile

different bikes all that easy, in that the Sunbeam tends to determine the speed at which you go.

Be prepared for extensive and expensive rebuilding but look forward to reliable – if unexciting – service when the bike is assembled and carefully set up.

Geoff Baker was the second person to be interviewed by the author, an S7 and S8 owner, and long-time enthusiast for these models:

GB: I saw my first-ever S7 in 1947 and immediately wanted one. I bought one in 1950 which I kept until 1957 and after that always fancied another. I now have both models.

RCC: When did you buy your S7, OHA 984?

GB: In 1973.

RCC: In what condition was the bike?

GB: Completely dismantled but basically complete.

RCC: What repair and renovation has been done?

GB: Not much, apart from paint and chrome. The mechanical parts were in pretty good nick and only wanted cleaning up. All the chrome was rusty, though, and the enamel was more or less useless. The bike needed minor new parts, cables and the like, but proved easy to assemble and runs well. I feel it's better to rebuild one than to buy one that may have been 'half-done' by someone else.

RCC: Have you experienced difficulty in obtaining parts?

GB: None at all. Everything is obtainable either from Stewart's or from old bike stockists.

RCC: What kind of performance and handling does the Sunbeam have?

RCC: Why are you so interested in the S7?

GB: Well, that very much depends on who you are. As you can see, I'm built for comfort not speed and the S7 is a bike in the same mould. I am not at all interested in going fast or playing racers and the bike fits me exactly for that reason. A good big 'un beats a good little 'un everytime! The S7 is safe and very comfortable; what more do you want in a bike?

RCC: What sort of use does your S7 get?

GB: Well, it's not in everyday use or anything like that. I use it when I feel like going for a ride on a motorcycle or for the odd local trip. It is handier than the car in the narrow lanes in my part of the world. It's a good bike in the wet, the big 'guards keep the mud off and it's very reliable.

RCC: Has your bike won any prizes in concours or similar events?

GB: Not really. I don't enter for that sort of thing.

RCC: Do you enter your S7 in any form of motorsport?

GB: Only local Vintage Club runs. I use it when I'm not on a proper vintage bike or when the run is for modern bikes. Very pleasant on a good day.

RCC: How helpful is it to be a member of the owners' club?

GB: Quite useful. Their magazine is a good one and the low subscription makes the Sunbeam Owners' Fellowship a worthwhile club for all owners.

RCC: How useful have you found the specialist parts suppliers?

GB: Very helpful. Stewart's prices sometimes make you blink but, as they point out, the bits cost about the same as those for a comparable Japanese bike. I know which I'd rather ride! They are very knowledgeable and usually happy to help on the 'phone if you are stuck.

RCC: How would you sum up the enjoyment you get from your S7?

GB: I bought the 'beam from a Mr Carter who had a 'thing' about Sunbeams and I can understand it. I have ridden them, as I say, for years, and had one tremendous smash on one, and I find that it's the bike that suits me. Only trouble is, the Sunbeam stays the same and I get older! I can't think of another bike that I would feel as happy on and that's what counts.

RCC: What advice would you give to potential owners of shaft-drive Sunbeams?

GB: Don't expect it to go like a racer. Try and ride one before you buy one, they don't suit everyone. Join the club and use the bike – if you just keep it in a garage as an 'investment' it's a waste of a good machine.

Super Profile

BUYING

Undoubtedly the S7 and S7 de luxe are more easily recognised and have much more charisma than the more prosaic S8, and thus command a higher price. Many potential owners search for an S7 model because of its apparent style and oddity.

The original S7 is a rare bird, particularly in original condition with its first series engine and gearbox, and is undoubtedly the sought-after machine. Mechanically, it is a much less satisfactory motorcycle than the two later models, and cannot be run satisfactorily in its catalogue specification unless driven very carefully due to the very low oil capacity of only three pints. Troubles with the Weiler chain tensioner and non-drainable (except by dismantling) final drive are also common. If the S7 is at all damaged or incomplete, finding the original parts will be a problem as much of the machine was unique and later parts from the S7 de luxe and S8 will not fit except by wholesale substitution.

In riding, the original S7 is less than satisfactory. The softly-sprung and completely undamped front and rear suspension allied to the bouncy saddle give a bouncy, choppy ride which, in combination with the imprecise steering and pronounced engine 'shake' at low speed found with the original engine mount system, can become uncomfortable and, occasionally, dangerous.

Having said all this, the S7 is a unique motorcycle, well worth having.

From 1949 the S7 de luxe and S8 bypass most of the problems. Both are eminently practical and comfortable motorcycles and can safely be ridden in crowded traffic or on major roads. Their major limitations were built into the design and are almost impossible to eradicate. The most serious is caused by the lubrication system, which is prone to cause oil leakage by virtue of the engine's poor breathing system, and this becomes apparent when indulging in sustained riding using speeds above 60 mph. The relatively low power output and the high weight of both cycles combine to restrict performance to a touring style.

The S7 de luxe has the BSA hydraulically-damped front fork and the standard BSA plunger rear suspension of the period. The forks are good, though a bit 'clashy', and control the bounce inherent in the large types reasonably well. The rear suspension is less satisfactory, but adequate. If fitted with the original saddle, comfort is paramount but a substitute dualseat shows up the bump and bounce to a surprising degree. The later style engine mounts smooth out the shake at the expense of the absolute turbine smoothness of the S7. The motor is mechanically much quieter than that of the S7 and even with a 'pattern' exhaust the bike's progress is as quiet as any Japanese 'multi'.

Spares for the later S7 are relatively easily obtainable from the specialist supplier, though they are not cheap as befits precision components made in small batches. Even an incomplete S7 de luxe can be restored to original specification both mechanically and 'bodily' with a minimum of frustration, and the result is a fine machine.

The S8 is altogether a more sporty package. Although the front and rear suspensions are the same as on the S7 de luxe, the narrower forks and different wheels give a completely different 'feel' to the ride. The simple saddle is easily replaceable and restoration is less of a problem even than the S7 de luxe. The use of standard tyres offers a choice of modern rubber and alternative wheel rims and the roadholding will always be superior to that of the de luxe. The rather weak S8 front brake can easily be removed and a later BSA one fitted, a 'mod' which considerably helps the stopping.

The almost complete lack of development and change in the models between 1949 and 1956 also contributes to the ease with which a '7' or '8' can be repaired.

Price patterns

The shaft-drive Sunbeam has never reached the extremely high figures asked for other famous British machines of the period and remains on a par, price-wise, with much more mundane bikes such as the BSA and Triumph twin ranges. The reasons are perhaps two-fold. The relatively low performance of the twins has gained them a sporting image which does not appeal to the harder rider or, for that matter, to

Super Profile

the rider who thinks he rides hard. Although problems with reliability are mostly in the past, the reputation lingers on amongst old riders.

Secondly, the twins are served by one parts supplier only and there is not the same facility to hunt for bargains in spares as there is with more common bikes. It must be said that Stewart Engineering have always been very fair with customers and that their work is good and reasonably priced, but the nervousness about part availability remains.

The early S7 comes on to the market so rarely that it is difficult to price and it has a genuine rarity value to collectors in that probably less than a hundred survive. It will fetch more than either the de luxe or S8 in the same condition.

Of the other two machines, the S7 de luxe commands a fractionally higher price, perhaps 10 – 15% more, than the S8. Although the S8 is a better handling, much easier restoration project, the S7 has that 'character' sought by collector's.

An incomplete or unrestored specimen will fetch less than half the price of a reasonable runner, itself probably only half the price of a 'concours' example, reflecting the availability and cost of spares. Insurance is the same as for any other 'collectors' 500 and performance potential rather less, also reflected in the price.

Selling is perhaps not as easy as for other collector's bikes, the Sunbeam appealing to a rather more restricted clientele. Above all, the Sunbeams are good for riding, and their failure to 'take off' in the price stakes is good news for all those discriminating riders who would like one. If you have the chance to buy one, think very hard before you turn it down! If it is an original S7, think even harder, or, better still, buy it.

The S7 has many problem areas. Later mechanical parts may not fit and repair of the forks and rear suspension may be very difficult or very expensive – and the suspension does not have the benefit of a good lubrication system. Mechanical noise may be higher and engine wear greater unless the lubrication system has been modified. A non-runner from the proverbial barn needs to be complete unless expert fabrication is available, or the owner is prepared to alter the specification.

On later bikes there are few major problems. The hubs and brakes can wear both in the drive splines and in the pressed drums, and the rear drive suffers both from wear caused by non-changing of the oil and by corrosion of the bronze wheel which shows up as a pitted surface. The 'land' between the tooth valleys should not be anything near the 'knife-edge' so often seen through the inspection plate. Never buy a shaft-drive Sunbeam without checking the worm wheel, for parts are very expensive.

Engine mounts can wear and perish but are easily and more or less cheaply replaceable and the camshaft and rockers can sound well enough but be worn enough to produce a marked lack of power. The distributor and dynamo are well-known danger areas and cures for both are available from Stewart's.

The gearbox is robust and well-designed, rarely giving much trouble and the driveshaft never gives trouble, though the front laminated joint is more likely to go than the rear metal universal joint. The bottom end of the engine is very strong, the oil-tightness often unsatisfactory unless a careful rebuild with the right modifications has been carried out.

The frame is difficult to bend, even in an accident, but the valances of the mudguards can rust badly. Happily, glassfibre replacements are generally available from Stewart's.

If an early S7 is not required, buy the latest and best S7 or S8 that you can find. If expense is a problem, mechanical restoration is more difficult and expensive than cosmetic work and can push up the price of a runner 'needing slight attention' to an unacceptable level.

The two later models can be found fairly easily. Very few weeks go by without examples being advertised in 'Motor Cycle Weekly', and the monthlies 'The Classic Motor Cycle' and 'Classic Bike' carry adverts and features on both machines. The Vintage Motor Cycle Club, the largest motorcycle club in the world, admits all three models to its ranks and many events cater for the shaft-drive twins, examples of which are often found in the VMCC Journal small-ad columns.

A 'wanted' advertisement in any of the above is almost certain to produce a response. There are still a few lurking in urban back yards and sheds, many having ground to a halt in the mid-sixties and an appeal in the local paper may well be a good idea.

Autojumbles often have secondhand spares and sometimes complete or incomplete examples, while the regular motorcycle and car auctions run by Sotheby's and Christie's frequently have examples available. Both auction houses will notify a potential purchaser of models appearing in forthcoming sales.

Super Profile

CLUBS, SPECIALISTS & BOOKS

While there are owners who are able to manage almost completely on their own, most of us find considerable advantages in belonging to either general or specialist clubs and in using the services of specialist manufacturers and authors. The amount of time and money to be saved by getting something done right from day one cannot be over-estimated and, though specialists have a right to charge for their services, their help is valuable in the extreme.

The club can provide help on a practical level and social and competitive events for the owner as well as the opportunity to meet with and learn from the experience of others. The specialist in parts and service has the equipment to make and install new components which the amateur, however well-equipped, would find difficult. The thought of making a worm and wheel set for a Sunbeam is enough to turn most of us in the direction of the specialist!

A book is a cheap way of finding out whether or not you want a Sunbeam, both the general histories and specific instruction books are essential reading before purchase and certainly so afterwards. Collectors may wish to obtain a set of the correct catalogues and books for their particular model and, to this end, a brief description of the 'works' publications is given.

Clubs

Sunbeam Owners' Fellowship

This is the only club exclusively for S7/S8 owners, holding meetings and rallies, as well as maintaining a register of known machines and a Technical Help service. A duplicated magazine, largely owner-based, is published at regular intervals containing articles of both technical and general interest. Worth the subscription.

Membership details from 'Rotor', c/o Stewart Engineering, 55, Bective Road, Putney, London, SW15 2QA – not at the Market Harborough address.

Vintage Motor Cycle Club

Originally formed to cater for vintage and veteran bikes made before 1930, the VMCC now embraces all machines made more than twenty-five years ago. All the shaft-drive Sunbeams are therefore eligible.

The VMCC is organised on a 'section' basis throughout the country and each section organises events, though not all of these cater for 'post-vintage' bikes. The members of the VMCC have a wealth of collective experience and it is rare to find a section where there is no member who knows about your bike. There is a monthly journal.
Membership Secretary –
K. Hallworth,
26, Shrigley Road North,
Higher Poynton,
Nr. Stockport,
Cheshire. SK12 1TE.

Specialists

In the S7 and S8 field there is one pre-eminent specialist, Stewart Engineering of Market Harborough. They make and factor a very wide range of mechanical and cosmetic spares and do work on Sunbeams as well as being a source of secondhand and reconditioned units. They are usually cheerful and helpful to owners who telephone. Their publications are excellent value.
Stewart Engineering,
PO Box 7,
Market Harborough,
Leicestershire.
LE16 8XL.
Tel. 0536 770962.

Books

'The Sunbeam Motorcycle'.
Robert Cordon Champ. Published by Haynes Publishing Group, Sparkford, Yeovil, Somerset, England.
A complete history of the Sunbeam make from cycles to the last scooters. Technical appendices and restoration guide. Biased towards the Marston Sunbeams by virtue of their length of production but there is a complete chapter on S7 and S8 models. 205 pages. Published by Haynes/Foulis in 1980.
'The Sunbeam Owner's Bedside Book'. Published by Stewart Engineering (q.v.) 90 pages. A most useful and entertaining combination of workshop manual and hints and tips directory. Guaranteed to produce insomnia if read last thing at night! Written by people who know about Sunbeams.
'Sunbeam Spares Catalogue'
Published by Stewart Engineering (q.v.). A catalogue of available spare parts and exchange assemblies from the country's premier specialists.

The following out of print books are fairly easily found at autojumbles or in secondhand bookshops and can be quite cheap and useful.

Sunbeam D.W. Munro.
Pearson Motor Cycle Repair and Maintenance Series 1954 138 pages. Contains all the data needed with many of the BSA diagrams and much material of the day.

Munro was involved in the development of the later S7 and S8 and this shows in this excellent book, the best for the early S7 owner.

The Book of the Sunbeam S7 and S8 W.C. Haycraft. (Pitman's Motor Cyclists Library. 1954 – reprinted several times) 120 pages.

More common than the Munro book this is readable and quite useful though not quite as good as its competitor. Covers all normal work on the Sunbeam in typical Haycraft/Pitman style.

BSA produced a Sunbeam catalogue each year. Unless you are a collector these are not worth having. Like most sales leaflets of the period they contain very little information and tend to command a high price.

The maker's instruction manual (red cover for S7 pre-1949, green cover subsequently) is a small-size, 70 page garage manual containing more technical information than problem-solving material. Pretty well all the contents are found in either the Haycraft or Monro books.

The S7 spare parts list, rather rare now – was again red-covered and small in size. Rather crude line drawings but absolutely essential for the addicts of the true S7. The later, post-1949, spares lists are large format and excellent, with good 'exploded' diagrams but with rather an awkward binding system.

BSA also produced a yearly data booklet of twelve small pages, presumably for dealers. These are of no importance to an owner, the information being contained in any instruction book.

Super Profile

PHOTO GALLERY

1. The old order ... Marston's Sunbeam wizard George Dance on a typically lightweight tourer of the 'twenties, in this case an ACU trial machine...

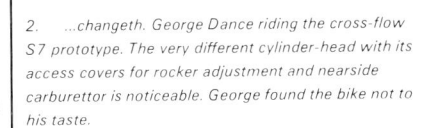

2. ...changeth. George Dance riding the cross-flow S7 prototype. The very different cylinder-head with its access covers for rocker adjustment and nearside carburettor is noticeable. George found the bike not to his taste.

3. A nearside view of the prototype 'fast' Sunbeam. Though much re-touched, the rocker covers and central camshaft access cover can be seen, as well as the large carburettor. Block-pattern tyres are fitted front and rear. (National Motor Museum).

4. Another S7 prototype, fitted with BMW-style looped, rigid frame. The engine is of the type fitted to production versions but is solidly mounted into the frame – the exhaust pipe has no flexible section and differs in having no 'elbows'.

Super Profile

5. Sunbeam designer Erling Poppe (with pipe) and Mr Nedham of BSA Redditch (with cigarette). The mounting holes over the dynamo have no obvious purpose and the rear number-plate mounting differs from production versions.

6. This is the final 'solid-engine' version of the S7 and is the one intended for sale, the photograph being taken from the S7 instruction book. The exhaust 'elbows' have appeared as has the tubular number-plate mounting and small rear light.

7. A very early S7, frame number S7-168 which the author rode for some years. The carburettor cover, tank and rear drive are non-original, typical of the 'mods' made to early S7s over the years.

8. The S7's most distinguished owner, Field Marshal The Viscount Montgomery, taking delivery of his S7 at the 1948 Earls Court show – so great was the rush to see the new Sunbeam that the show stand collapsed under the weight.

Super Profile

9. A surviving S7, CFK 333 (the owner hadn't noticed the wrong number!) The exhaust pipe now has its flexible section and the bracing bar sits under the dynamo. The rear light is not original.

10. The nearside view shows the front horn mounting and the absence of a prop-stand. The tank is identical in shape to later S7s. The special 'twistgrip' made for the S7 is missing - it proved to be unreliable in use.

Super Profile

11. The fluted alloy tank-cap screws into the early S7 tank. The early air-cleaner cover conceals a modern Amal and the engine breather is a Stewart fitting.

12. The early S7 gearbox has differently spaced mounting studs and the access cover is louvred. The different shapes of the head and block castings can be seen, as well as evidence of hand-filed castings at BSA.

13. The S7's forks are unique in their use of a brace between lugs on the fork sliders and a central spring unit. The fork bushes are not easily repairable. The top caps spring out to allow the internal cotton wool to be soaked in oil.

14. The S7's rear frame is built from tube and lugs and the footrest mounting is at the bottom. The top caps are again for oil-wick wetting. Early rear-drive units had no drain plugs, most have been replaced.

Super Profile

15. Inverted levers are comfortable and protect the hands in a crash, but are expensive to make. A legacy from the nineteen-twenties, they are standard on early S7s. The original twistgrip was of the straight-pull internal cable type.

16. The early air-cleaner successfully kept in the engine's heat, much to the discomfort of the carburettor, bolted directly to the 25 mm inlet port of the cylinder head. The exhaust elbows, of iron on early S7s, did not help.

17. The S7 de luxe, the final development of the S7, in production from 1949 - 1956. Front forks have standard BSA internals and rear suspension is re-designed.

18. Nearside view shows the standard propstand and differently shaped stand legs, the ratchet of the S7 having been dropped. The frame, through, is still finished in black.

19. A polished and chromed S7 at a rally. Engine/gearbox/brake/drive castings left the works in an unpolished state.

20. Somewhat modernised, this S7 sports a sealed beam headlight, winkers, and the more usual crash-bars and pannier set. The rear lifting handle is not Sunbeam but should have been!

33

Super Profile

21.

22.

23.

21. GJU 341 again. The shape of the S7 can 'absorb' bulky equipment without ruining its looks. Many have been turned into pseudo Harleys, though.

22. Pump mounting is standard, but removal is advised when leaving the bike. The S7 after 1949 had the standard bayonet-fitting tank cap of so many other makes.

23. The later S7 and S8 'snubber' between engine and frame. The larger rubber after 1949 makes the engine feel smoother but the clearance is still critical, hence the thread and lock-nut adjustment. The small bolt secures the steel crankcase boss.

Super Profile

24. Offside view of the special Lucas distributor. The plate behind it is part of the friction damper anchored to the top-tube to control engine movement. The distributor is well protected from wet weather.

25. The slot and nut adjustment for timing is clearly shown here, as well as some of the corrosion that can attack the aluminium-alloy casing of the distributor. At least Lucas didn't use zinc alloy.

26. The cylindrical spring-stop for the chain tensioner is on the left. The cover is removed for cam-chain adjustment. The clutch cable is routed through the steady on the gearbox casing.

27. The double spring holds down the combined dipstick and filler cover. At high engine revolutions the crankcase pressure can lift the cap, causing oil leaks.

28. The simple, standard controls, fitted to later Sunbeams. The clutch lever in particular needs a strong pivot, notably lacking in these levers.

35

Super Profile

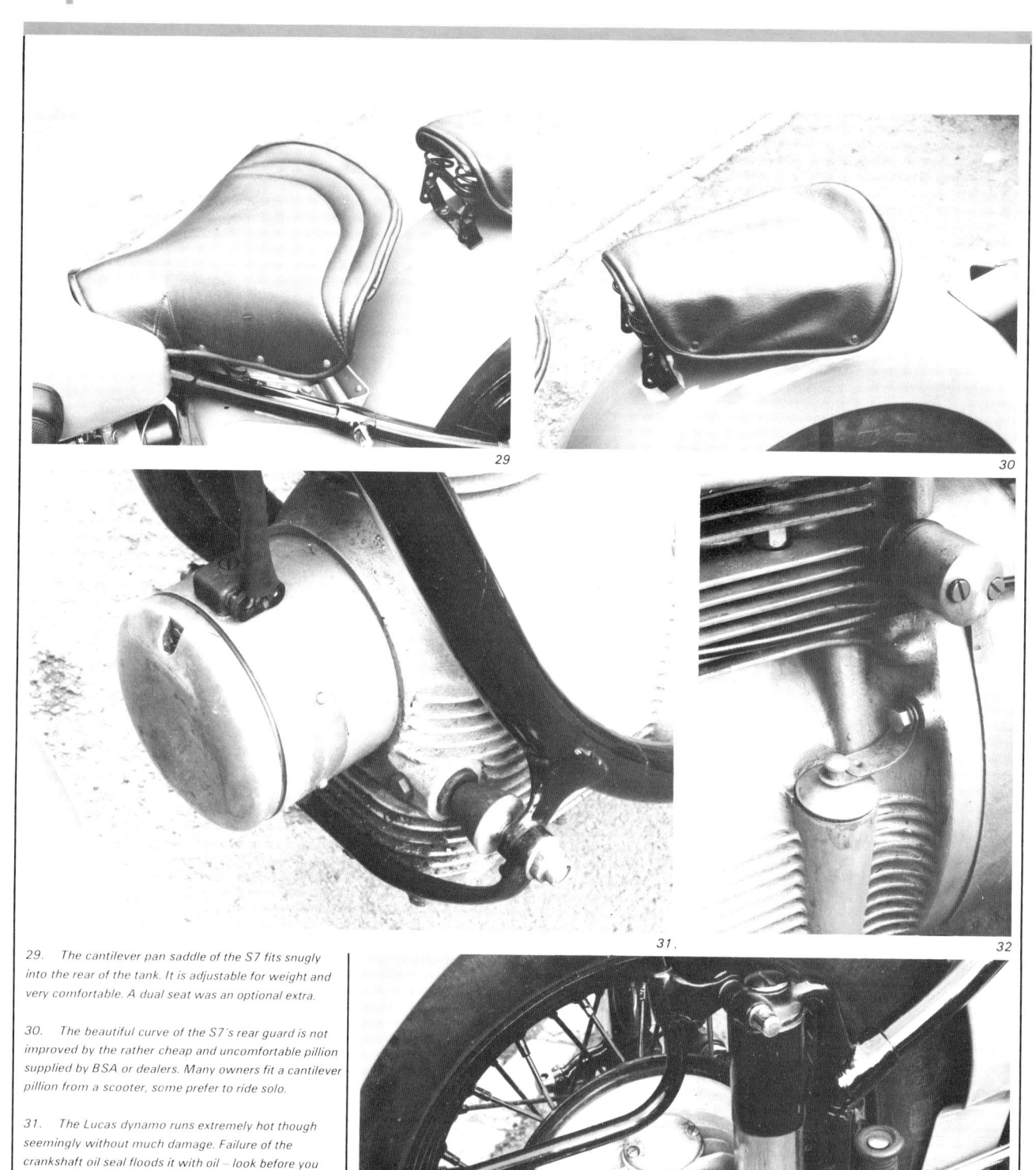

29. The cantilever pan saddle of the S7 fits snugly into the rear of the tank. It is adjustable for weight and very comfortable. A dual seat was an optional extra.

30. The beautiful curve of the S7's rear guard is not improved by the rather cheap and uncomfortable pillion supplied by BSA or dealers. Many owners fit a cantilever pillion from a scooter, some prefer to ride solo.

31. The Lucas dynamo runs extremely hot though seemingly without much damage. Failure of the crankshaft oil seal floods it with oil – look before you buy! The connector is flimsy and inadequate.

32. The cylinder head is secured by nuts hidden between the fins, only able to be tightened with an open-ended spanner. Head gaskets are prone, therefore, to leak oil and compression if not tightened carefully.

33. The later one-piece casting of the suspension bracket – internals are standard BSA. The securing bolt for the mudguard stay is released by tommy-bar.

Super Profile

34. The nearside suspension assembly shows the tommy bar fittings for the spindle, pinch bolt and mudguard. Only a tommy bar is needed to remove either wheel on a Sunbeam – something which modern bikes could well copy.

35. The offside box contains the electrical components. Quite why the ammeter and light switch were put here is difficult to understand but they are less likely to be damaged by weather – as the car-type switch is not waterproof, this helps a lot.

36. Another thoughtful touch for the rider is the provision of a set of spare bulb holders in the electric box. The speedometer cable runs through the box but accessibility to electrical components is good.

Super Profile

37. Both footrest and brake pedal are well-made and adjustable for rider comfort. Coin-slotted screws give access to the toolbox, a very roomy and useful fitting appreciated by riders, un-noticed by poseurs.

38. The (feeble) Altette horn mounts on to the frame, the propstand also, both lugs being brazed on. The gearbox is dismantled through the side-plate behind the toolbox, the joint being prone to leak unless Allen screws are used.

Super Profile

39. The exhaust elbows are rather prone to thread stripping unless carefully used. The brass nuts on the block face and the C-spanner sleeve nuts are both prone to damage unless carefully handled.

40. The cold start plunger is visible behind the air cleaner shield, though this carb, is a later Amal. It is preferable to use armoured petrol-piping near to the exhaust pipes!

41. Engine number is visible next to the gearbox level plug. All post 1949 S7s and S8s have an S8 prefix. The inner chrome bezel of the gear change rotates to indicate the gear engaged.

42. The alloy fork top shrouds incorporate the push-in tax disc holder while the lower shrouds are secured by three small screws. The headlamp varies in detail from the early pattern.

Super Profile

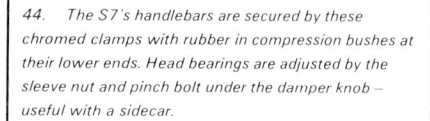

43. Driver's-eye view. The wide spread of the S7 forks can be seen here as can the car-type warning lights and Chronometric speedometer.

44. The S7's handlebars are secured by these chromed clamps with rubber in compression bushes at their lower ends. Head bearings are adjusted by the sleeve nut and pinch bolt under the damper knob — useful with a sidecar.

45. The Teutonic appearance of the forks is a carry-over from the BMW via the early S7. Fork tubes and sliders are typically BSA. The number-plate can smash the headlamp glass on full depression if it is not kept to a small size.

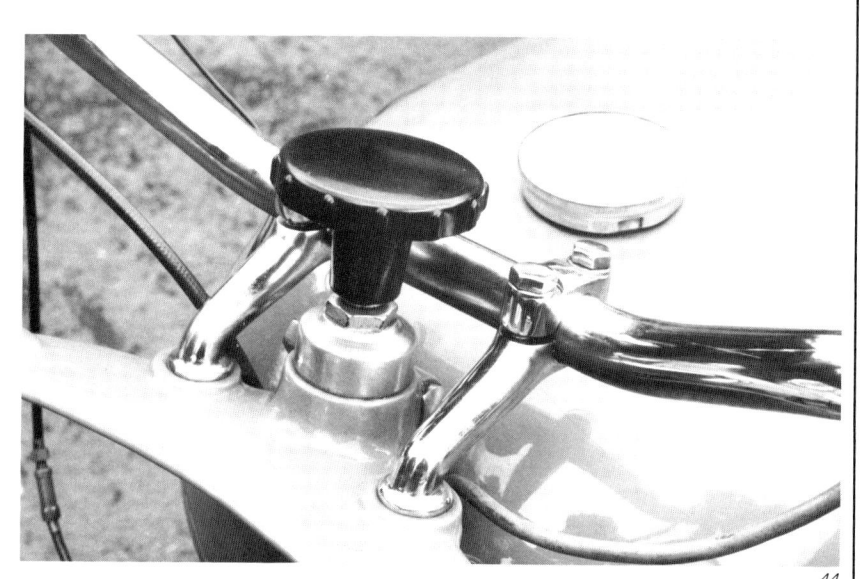

Super Profile

46. Part of the staggering variety of fasteners used on the S7 forks – very interesting but expensive to produce. The top nuts are identical to those on other BSA machines.

47. Front wheel spindle and pinch-bolt. As with the rear wheel, no spanners are needed for wheel removal. The rear mudguard stay doubles as a front stand in the normal way.

48. The massive fork, guard and wheel assembly of the S7 makes for slightly imprecise steering and can affect the bike's progress in cross-winds. The forks are typical period BSA in action and comfort.

49. The continental-style front brake of the S7 is a beautiful casting, though the internal operating arms are not over-stiff. Equipped with a totally protected mechanism and simple squared adjuster, this is another trouble-free feature of the S7.

Super Profile

50. The S7 shows off its weight and size in comparison to its younger brother, the S8. Both current from 1949, the S8 scored on sales to people nervous about the S7's apparent size. The width of the S7 forks is most noticeable.

51. From the rear the difference is less apparent. The S8 has a wider mudguard for its tyre size than the S7 and the frame width is identical.

Super Profile

52.

53.

52. A BSA publicity photograph of the 1952 S8 – not that the year makes much difference. This is the 'Polychromatic Gun Metal Grey' finish. Note the Dunlop Universal tyres front and rear.

53. Another BSA photograph of the S8. 'Sunbeam' appears on the air-cleaner cover. The front brake has a chromed backplate and is the same miserable stopper fitted to some other post-war BSA models.

43

Super Profile

54. A close-up of the S8 engine unit reveals that it is identical in all respects to that of the S7 de Luxe.

55. A well-restored S8 reveals the much more fashionable 'slimline' look. The S8 has improved standards of roadholding and, of course, a much wider choice of tyres. Wheel rims and front brake are non-original in this case.

Super Profile

56

56. The S8 front forks are virtually standard BSA as fitted to other models of the period and can now be much improved with a few internal changes to seals and damping rates and fluids. Tax disc-holder is now the usual bolt-on device.

57. The brake lever is internally splined and also

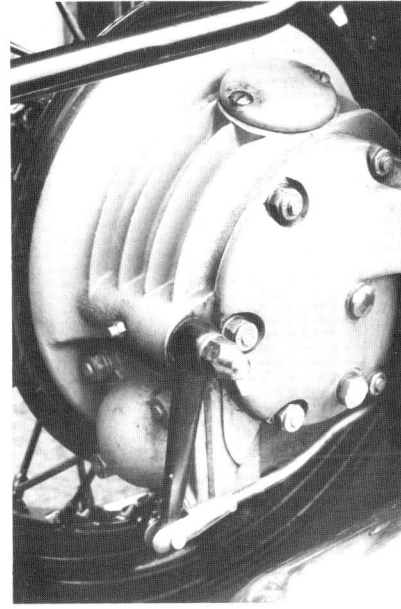

57

adjustable by means of the threaded rod. This and the wheel are pinched up tight by the thread of the spindle seen protruding through the case. Check the worm wheel through the top cover.

58. The rear number plate fitting is, again, standard BSA instead of the tubular light housing on the S7.

58

Correct rear light specifications are given in the technical section.

59. S8 tank is identical to that on the S7. Tank kneegrips are a standard John Bull pattern, still available. Modern motorcyclists prefer to rest their knees on shiny paint.

59

Super Profile

60. The S8 saddle is a standard three-point fixing model used on many other machines. The frame mounting is different from that of the cantilever S7 saddle, an easy frame identification point.

61. The most noticed feature of the S8 is its beautiful cast-alloy silencer with separate inlet and outlet pipes, both constricted for some silence and thus easily opened out. Beware of cracks and other damage.

Super Profile

62.

63.

64.

62. This is the brake that should have been fitted to the S8 in the first place! Used on various BSA singles and twins it bolts straight into the S8 forks without modification and provides first-class stopping.

63. Offside view of the BSA experimental water-cooled four-cylinder engine used in a now badly-damaged works prototype. The Amal carburettor and S7 front engine mount are visible.

64. Nearside view of the experimental four-cylinder. The flywheel is standard S7/8 and the small size of the unit can be seen by comparison with the normal car-type distributor fitted.

65. Nippon Sunbeam! Tank badge of the Japanese Liner TW still has the crown inherited from the Marston Sunbeam emblem.

65.

47

Super Profile

66. Nearside view of the Liner 250 cc engine-gear unit. Obvious differences are the BMW-style kickstarter and the left side foot-change lever, but its ancestry is very obvious. (Jens Evang).

67. Offside view of the Liner TW. The crudity of the brake pedal is surprising as is the 1930s-style fabric universal joint. Otherwise it's a case of 'spot the similarity'. (Jens Evang).

68. The Liner TW, photographed in Japan. Later versions had a beam-type frame but the overall styling is Sunbeam S8 with just a touch of Triumph. They didn't fall for the worm-drive trap, though copying most of the Sunbeam's ideas. (Jens Evang).

Super Profile

C1. The early S7 Comparatively few of these machines remain and all were originally finished in black. The main identification points are the front forks, the inverted lever controls and the frame's different construction. The aluminium air-cleaner cover is now a rare item.

C2. It is difficult to judge whether the bulk of the S7 was increased or diminished by the black paint. In this shot, the plug cover has been removed. The similarity to a wartime BMW is very apparent, though, understandably, BSA made no mention of it. The tyre sizes prevent wheel interchangeability.

49

Super Profile

C3. The more familiar S7 de Luxe in its Mist-Green paintwork with more normal telescopic forks. In this well-restored example the use of black frame and wheels is standard BSA practice, as are the cantilever saddle and ovoid air-cleaner cover. Silencer external shape is almost identical to that of the nineteen-fifties Gold Star.

C4. The Mist-Green paint certainly brightens up the S7 de Luxe's less exciting profile. The comments made by other riders about 'tractor tyres' can be understood from this viewpoint, the machine unfortunately looking much heavier than it really is.

Super Profile

C5. The complete engine-gear unit of the S7 de Luxe showing the kickstarter and gear pedal, the latter direct on to the shaft, necessitating a steep downward angle for most people. The flexible exhaust pipe made essential by the rubber-mounted engine is a common source of leaks and fractures!

C6. The smooth appearance of the S7's 'power egg' can be seen. The dynamo is mounted BMW-style on the crankcase nose and the bracing bar between the crankcase rubbers can be seen. The sump capacity has been increased since the S7's inception – compare with CFK 333.

C7. The beautiful swell of the S7's rear guard entirely suits the character of the bike. The tubular number plate support is unchanged from that of the early S7 when it housed a small, round lamp. Glassfibre copy guards are available.

Super Profile

C8. The headlamp contains the flanged Smiths 120 mph speedometer with trip milometer – an 80 mph version was fitted on the early S7. The oil and charge warning lights are almost identical to those fitted on Rover P4 cars. Hexagon fork nuts identify BSA forks.

C9. The engine breather cover can be seen at the front of the cambox. It contains three spring-loaded disc breathers. The standard modification is an alloy 'box' with a breather pipe routed downwards. Below and to the right of the breather is the first rubber mounting.

C10. The badge echoes very strongly the original 'The Sunbeam' badge of the old John Marston Sunbeams. It is enamelled metal, secured to a loop on the tank recess by a spring steel clip. The original colour for the early S7 was blue, yellow coming in 1949.

Super Profile

C11. The S8 introduced in 1949 had this silver 'Polychromatic Gun Metal Grey' as the alternative to the black finish. Always better-looking without a pillion seat, the mudguard's silver-grey and the aluminium of the engine and silencer harmonise well together. The front brake is non-original but of BSA design.

C12. Even in silver-grey the nearside remains visually much more dull than the offside. The S8, though, has a smoothness of appearance and performance totally lacking in most English machines of the period.

Super Profile

C13. This is a beautifully restored S8 in black, fitted with alloy wheel rims and the later BSA front brake. The pillion seat is a standard item which breaks up the line of the mudguard.

C14. The elegance and finish of the Poppe-designed Line-Ahead Twin contrasts with the black of the tank and frame. The front breather is a modified one and the exhaust nuts are the pattern now supplied by Stewart Engineering.

C15. Mechanically identical to both S7 de Luxe and black S8, the example here has original exhaust nuts. The close proximity of the carburettor to the exhaust pipes can give problems due to fuel evaporation.

Super Profile

C16. The alloy plug-cover protects the leads and plugs from rain in an effective fashion. This machine has the brass extension pipe for the oil-pressure sensor in order to cool the switch — a works modification.

C17. The silencer tailpipe is secured by a pinch-bolt through the alloy casting. If the tailpipe crushes, the silencer splits! The cover with four nuts is used for shimming the worm to correct mesh with the wheel, in conjunction with the front access housing.

55

Super Profile

C18. The alloy silencer was a bold design, unique to the S8. Largely without internal baffles, it gives a splendidly sporty exhaust note. Although the drive-shaft appears small in diameter, breakages are virtually unknown though joint couplings can fail and are expensive.

C19. The rear-drive unit is prone to overheat and can suffer badly from wear and corrosion. The rod linkages for the brake were chromed as standard, as was the rear-wheel spindle whose end can be seen in the centre of the unit, being screwed through from the nearside.